Growing Together

....

Understanding and Nurturing Your Child's Faith Journey

by Anne Neufeld Rupp

F&L
FAITH & LIFE
P R E S S

Newton, Kansas
Winnipeg, Manitoba

Second printing 1998

Printed in the United States of America.

International Standard Book Number 0-87303-238-1
Library of Congress Number 95-83740

Editorial direction by Susan E. Janzen; editing by Helen Johns; copy-
editing by Mary L. Gaeddert; design by John Hiebert; printing by
Mennonite Press, Inc. Cover art by Joy Dunn Keenan.

Contents

Introduction

The years with our children are like a journey through a woods where green things grow. Journey imagery suggests growth: growth toward maturation of our faith and the emotional, moral, and spiritual growth of our children. Parenting is an adventure, like a journey on paths through thickets and trees where we can't always anticipate what lies ahead. Sharing our faith with those entrusted to us is an even greater adventure. In either case, we can't retrace our steps and we can't outpace our children. The time we have with them is not the months past or the years ahead. We only have *now,* this present moment, to guide and lead our young ones.

When we acknowledge how much of parenting depends on grace, we become less uptight and more hopeful about our task. We parents are responsible, but we are not alone nor does everything rest on our shoulders. We make mistakes because we are human, but through forgiveness (sometimes we have to ask it of our children) we experience grace. We recognize that God works miracles in us (and in our children), through us, and despite us on days when our own faith seems unrelated to what's happening in our everyday world. With God's help and the guidance of the Holy Spirit, we do our very best and believe that a Greater Power carries us and our children from there on.

So ours is a journey of hope. We can invest in hope for ourselves and hope for our children because of God's almighty grace. And emerging as a result of hope are deeper love, joy, and an inner calm—essential ingredients for parenting and sharing a live faith with our children.

In this book we will focus on the tasks of parenting and sharing our faith with children from infancy to preadolescence. This emphasis needs to be understood within the context of *our own* beginning and end and *our own* growth towards fuller maturity in Jesus Christ. A thirty-nine-year-old man said to me, "I don't need to learn any more about faith; I know all I need to know." He was operating on the assumption that faith is a fact, something you attain and hold. Faith is not something we *own*—it is a gift. Through the power of God's Spirit, our experiences, and learning, faith that begins as tiny as a mustard seed grows to a faith that can move mountains.

Sharing faith with our children begins with looking at our own faith. Someone has said that the gospel is one beggar telling another beggar where to find bread. But if we haven't found the bread or tasted the warm, crusty morsels, how can we share it with another? The challenge for parents to experience and grow in faith underlies each chapter in this book.

The parental responsibility of sharing faith may seem overwhelming. "I've never learned how!" "I haven't been trained for this!" We stammer our fears and wish the church would take over. Some of us bravely say, "Yes, I want to share my faith with my children." But in our technological society, we look for a recipe or instruction book that we can follow step-by-step to turn out a product to our liking. But children aren't machines, tools, or even angel food cakes. They more resemble the variety found in God's nature than static objects who we assume will respond if we do it "right." Faith doesn't have an instruction manual. Faith is an experience, not a fact; a verb, not a noun. It can't be the same experience for everyone. In this book I will repeatedly stress that there is no single way to engage children in life and faith, but I will give you guidelines to help you understand your children, yourself, and your faith. Suggestions are made for nurturing the faith lives of your children in ways they can understand.

In stressing faith, I am not minimizing religion. When I say, "We can teach religion, but we can't teach faith," I don't undervalue religious instruction. But because it's easier to engage in the former than live the latter, I am placing a special emphasis on the faith dimension. In this book I state that religious instruction is the cradle in which the faith infant is laid and the guide who nourishes that infant. Thus, as you share faith as naturally as you breathe and live, you will also receive instruction for teaching religion, ethics, morals, values, and so on, to your child in age-appropriate ways.

Finally, I want to remind all of us that sharing faith with those young ones God has entrusted to our care is not a one-sided experience. It involves God, us, and the child. It is not a one-time or weekly event; it is a daily venture of growth and new possibilities. If we think we have all the answers, we may actually have very few. Faith is not static; it is an experience and a life lived. That's why we use more than verbal methods. We keep our eyes, ears, and spiritual minds and hearts open. We may be surprised at how often our children's simple faith can teach us to grow with them. Their innocent remarks are not to be laughed at even though they may appear cute. If we take them seriously, our own lives may be full of new spiritual surprises. This is the challenge for us as parents, our special form of ministry to those who come after us—the next generation.

The thirteen chapters in this book encompass the life cycle from infancy to preadolescence. To emphasize the dynamic dimension of faith, I have written from the perspective of a journey through a forest with numerous diverging paths to choose from, patches of many-hued wildflowers, trees reaching for the sky, brambles and underbrush, birds overhead. Unexpected twists and turns and shifts in wind or weather may change our plans and directions, and surprise us with things least expected.

Sharing life and faith within the family is a journey filled with surprises, unexpected turns, joy, sorrow, love, pain, and possibility. May you experience growth, grace, and hope during these important years with your young children.

How To Use this Book

....

This book is intended for both home and church use. It is a guidebook for caregivers of young children, regardless of parental age, marital status, or family size. The aim is to empower parents or other caregivers to live and share their faith with their children. Each chapter begins with an observation or experience in nature, each one representing some aspect of faith life with your children. This opening is followed by the main body, which is divided into a series of topics based on questions, and concludes with an excerpt called **Travel tips**. These divisions make it possible for parents to read one part at a time, pursue other segments later, or select those parts that relate to their particular concerns or questions.

Three other divisions follow the main section.

For review and response contains **Recap**, a brief overview of the main body, and **What then shall we do?**, which provides practical helps.

For family includes activities related to the chapter topic for **Family time**, holiday-related experiences in **Celebrate the family** (these activities may be used with any chapter), and **An idea for a family night activity**.

Finally, **For study** contains **Search the Scriptures**, a brief Bible study, **Discuss the questions**, an idea to help a family or study group **Engage in group response**. Here are some ways parents, families, and study groups might use these various sections:

Parents: Study the content and refer to **Recap**. For personal faith growth, engage in **What then shall we do?**

Family: Involve your children by selecting from **For family**. Because not all activities are theme, church year, or season related, I've included three indexes at the end of the book that may prove helpful: **Index for family time**, **Index for celebrate the family**, and **Index for family night activities**.

Groups: I suggest studying the materials at home. When you get together as a group, follow the guidelines under **For study**. **Discuss the questions** raises issues directly related to the chapter's main segments. You may want to open or close the group time with prayer.

These sections are flexible. Parents who are not part of a study group may want to use additional materials from **For study** for their own further growth. A study group may want to help participants select appropriate age-related family activities from **For family** or even do some of these activities together, thereby creating a small support community. Families may want to use the Scripture references from **For study** as a basis for family meditations, and develop related activities:

For fact learning: Make verbal statements and ask children to fill in the blanks (or for older children, write some fill-in-the-blank questions).

For memorization: Make a rebus (write the reference on newsprint but substitute pictures for the nouns).

For involvement: All ages paint or draw what the story says to them.

For experience: Involve the family directly in life-related experiences, for example, visiting a family with a new baby (chapter 3) or touring local churches (chapter 2 or 13).

The thirteen chapters in this book are not all-inclusive. Many more parenting topics could be discussed. I urge you to read a wide variety of periodicals and books found in your bookstore or library. The bibliography at the back of this book suggests additional resources. Read not only about children and faith but also study materials that will enhance your personal faith. Share with other parents. Participate in an active, welcoming church community. Study the Scriptures.

Make faith growth a high priority, because it is precisely out of your life and experience that your young children will learn about and experience faith.

Chapter 1

The Family Tree

Who and How I Became on the Way to Growing Up

....

Preparing for the journey

No parent is perfect. If we were, we wouldn't need God. But we do. Time and again, we need God quite desperately. Do you think our parents ever felt that way? our grandparents? The faith of parents and their parents and their parents all the way back to the first century has sustained Christianity and empowered families with the abundant life that Jesus promises to give. Now it's up to us. Our generation. Where do we start?

In this chapter you and your children will begin a journey through the woods. The word "journey" suggests that the years with our children are not static but dynamic, with many twists and curves in the road leading to surprises, joys, and, not infrequently, pain and suffering. Woods are not always as serene as they appear at the outset. On this excursion into the woods you will be communicating your faith life to those young ones who have been entrusted to you.

Before you set out, ask yourself several questions. After all, much of this book is about you and how your faith life touches your children.

What is faith?

The pages in this book are like a road map that guides you on your journey through the woods. They will help you explore ways to share your faith with the young ones entrusted to you. But before you get immersed in too many details, we must begin with the word "faith" and some understanding of what we're talking about.

First, a definition of what faith is not. Faith is not religion. Religion is not faith. Too readily we confuse the two. Religion and faith are not clones; they are more like kissing cousins. We can be highly religious yet only have a nodding acquaintance with faith. But faith *cannot* be a foreign object or occasional visitor in our lives. It is all consuming. Religion can be taught, but faith cannot. Faith is an existential experience, a relationship with God through Jesus Christ, lived daily. The gospel is good news that can be shared, witnessed to, and lived. But the moment we tell another, "You must do this and this and then you will have faith," we destroy the mustard seed (Matthew 17:20) because faith is not concrete. You can't see, taste, smell, or handle it. Faith always contains an element of uncertainty, otherwise it would not be faith.

Religion and faith are both important. Parents in Israel were instructed to teach God's commands, decrees, and laws to their children from generation to generation (Deuteronomy 6:6-9). Through this religious teaching they were providing a climate in which faith could be born. Religious instruction is the cradle in which the faith infant sleeps or the manger within which the Incarnate is laid. And if ever we needed religious instruction, including the teachings of the Bible, values, morals, or respect for human life and the environment, it is today and tomorrow. Many parts of this book will be devoted to helping you create this context by illustrating ways to teach your children about God in age-appropriate ways. But the essence of each chapter will focus on expressions and experiences of faith—yours and the child's.

What then is faith?

Now that we've clarified that faith and religion are both important but are not the same thing, let's go back to the question, "What is faith?"

Faith is God coming to us and surprising us with a sudden nativity. We may diligently search for God, but faith is not something we can take or demand. It is a gift of God's grace. When God touches us and calls us, we come alive, we respond. We suddenly recognize that Jesus Christ is indeed the Way, the Truth, and the Life. Have you seen the painting of the creation by Michelangelo? It shows God's arm and hand reaching down to the emerging human who is reaching out. As their fingertips touch, that creation becomes adam (humanity), a living being, energized by the breath of God. That's how it is with faith.

Faith is an experience, a daily live meeting with God that makes a difference in how one lives, acts, and converses. In the Deuteronomy passage, religious instruction is mandated and is presented within the context of faith (6:4-5). The writer makes four statements about parental faith: (1) Faith of the parent is demonstrated through love; loving God with all one's heart, soul, and mind; (2) faith is lived in a commitment that takes priority over all else morning, noon, and night; (3) faith is expressed through action, symbolism, and visible participation in raising the God awareness of the next generation; and (4) faith is lived and shared in community. God addresses a people; it is not an isolated experience. Faith begins at home and is shared, recognized, and affirmed within the community of believers.

Faith cannot be simply defined; it has both the simplicity and complexity of a kaleidoscope with its many-splendored sides, shapes, and sizes. It is experienced and perceived differently by different people in different cultures and at different ages. For some, coming to faith is an emotional experience. For others, it is more rational. For some, it's an abrupt change of life direction (repentance means "to turn around"). For others, it is a transition or even a process rooted in early childhood faith. In Acts we have examples of both individuals and whole households responding to the good news of Jesus Christ. Look at the gospels and see how Jesus called respondents to faith in a variety of ways and places. We cannot limit faith responses to only one view of conversion. A limitless God has many paths, and on one of these this Divine One will find us.

Faith is not something you possess—it possesses you. You do not wake up one morning and say, "Aha, now I have faith." Faith requires ongoing renewal and growth. It demands our whole being and a whole lifetime. But the *focus of faith* begins and remains consistent. Faith is expressed in a life and trust that professes, "God is my Creator and Jesus Christ is my redeeming Savior and Lord, now and through eternity."

Do we have faith?

A few years ago, John Westerhoff wrote a book titled *Will Our Children Have Faith?* Perhaps to get at the root of faith life, we do well to retitle the book with our second question, "Do We Parents Have Faith?" Do we have a maturing trust in Jesus Christ as Lord and Savior, and a dynamic Christian life empowered by God's Spirit? The faith of our children begins with the ways these young ones perceive and experience us. That's why it's important to begin with ourselves—by recognizing our uniqueness before God and identifying the nature of our personal faith and trust.

I have often wondered who I would be if I weren't me. What are the destinies that bring two people together? Revolutions and wars have ended many love relationships, and these individuals ended up marrying another. How would life have been different if that historical crisis had not occurred? Or even more simply, if your family was mobile or your parents met in the same college, how did these environments create the possibility of love and marriage that would have been different if each had married the boy or girl next door? You either believe in chance, or (more likely) in the free will of the human individual whose particular choices at that time, even though they easily could have been different in another environment, are God's opportunity to work all things for good. The belief that God is personally interested in us affirms our self-worth, empowers our faith, and makes it possible for us to be loving, caring people who are able to communicate that faith to the next generation.

You and I are God's unique beings, created in the divine image for love and relationships, redeemed through God's beloved son, Jesus Christ. That's God's investment in us. How we respond in trust and how we feel about ourselves is our part. Both are critical elements in communicating our faith. Our children will see in us not what we say but who we are and what we do—how we handle our own feelings and emotions, our problems, our stresses, our decisions, and our relationships.

And in the middle of this, we must never for a moment forget that through God's grace we have been gifted with a specialness that makes us unique. That's something no one can take from us, even during moments when our world appears to fall apart. That's what our children will see in us. That's how the energy forces of our faith will reach out to them and empower and enrich their lives. So in the end, only you can answer the questions: What is the nature of my faith experience, granted so graciously by a loving God? If faith is a trust relationship, empowered by God, how do I nurture this union? If I stepped into the shoes of my child, how would that child describe my faith?

How was faith communicated at home?

Faith doesn't come to us in a vacuum. It is transmitted or caught like a flu bug (but in a positive sense). After twenty centuries of passing on Christian faith—of generating faith from generation to generation—we can safely assume that much of the time these influences, both negative and positive, occurred within the family.

The home where you grew up and the caregivers in that home were the first experiences that shaped your idea of God. The faith experiences (or lack thereof) that we were exposed to during childhood influenced us more than we know. We may not be aware how those events affected us negatively or positively. You may negate your past and declare, "I will never be like that!" yet find yourself fighting your mother or father all your life in the way you relate to your spouse or children. Coming to grips with hurting experiences is important, for only then can you find the freedom from yourself and your past that allows you to experience the Christian faith in all its fullness. But it is equally or even more important to think about the positive dynamics of your childhood. Reflect on your growing-up years and ask yourself, "How was faith communicated in the home where I grew up?"

My parents were young people when they migrated to

Canada in the 1920s. They met, married, and raised a family. I'm the oldest child. That's a simple statement, but the reality is that like mobile families of today adjusting to different settings, environments, and even cultures, this young family was making a major transition from one way of life to another. Small wonder that there were tensions and struggles. But the amazing thing is that the faith life of my parents overrode the stresses. My mother, orphaned early, was the symbol of love and compassion in our family, and that's how I experienced God. I couldn't understand an eight-year-old friend who cried because she was afraid of hell. Jesus loved me the way my mother loved me; there was nothing to be afraid of. My father was an itinerant minister who farmed and then was gone, sometimes a month at a time, preaching in churches throughout the country. I felt the insecurity often sensed by children today whose parent is consistently absent. Yet when he came home and I saw that light in his face and heard his joy when he spoke about his ministry, that commitment and joy offset all else. Even today, as I assess my relationship with God, it can best be expressed by how I experienced the faith of my parents: love, joy, and commitment.

Now look at your own experience. By being aware of how the faith of the previous generation influenced you, you will also have more insight about how your children may be reading you.

How was religious instruction effected at home?

As noted earlier, faith is an experience that is caught rather than taught. A well-known theologian once said, "The gospel is not there to make us good, it is there to make us joyful!" In Jesus' parables about the lost son, the lost sheep, and the lost coin, the central theme was the joy of homecoming (Luke 15). Paul, though in prison, counseled his parishioners at Philippi with the words "Rejoice in the Lord always" (4:4). Joy is the first expression of faith. Goodness is a by-product of that joy. We want to live by Jesus' guidelines for life, not only because it's the best way to live but also because this is our response of gratitude to a God who has adopted us into the divine royal family (Romans 8:14-17). It's the lifestyle expected of royalty.

But goodness cannot be assumed. It must be taught and modeled as evidenced by the Sermon on the Mount and the closing chapters in Paul's epistles. That is the religious training mentioned earlier. So the earlier imagery shifts. Religious instruction is not only the cradle in which faith may be born but also the guide that helps that faith infant grow toward maturity in Christ (Ephesians 4:10-13).

As you reflect on your growing up, what was the nature of religious instruction in your home? How much of this theology, these values, this sense of right and wrong dominates your current life and thinking? What have you changed? What would you want to pass on or teach differently to your children?

How many generations have influenced my faith?

The family of God is a huge family. Horizontally, it numbers thousands upon thousands throughout the continents of our world. Vertically, it encompasses generations of faith people stretching back through the centuries. We are all part of a larger history; each one of us is a walking history book. So another important question to ask is "How much of what my caregivers passed on was part of their own parent's influence and witness? How did that affect me?"

My mother grew up in a Siberian village. Times were hard for the young homesteaders. My grandfather was drafted into forestry service, leaving grandmother to raise five young children. When my mother was seven, her mother suddenly became ill and died. A few hours before her death, she called her children to her bedside and prayed for and with each one. Seven years later, grandfather died, and he also called the children to his bedside and prayed with them. Through all her years, my mother repeatedly told me, "The prayers of my parents have sustained me throughout life." I, in turn, was touched and influenced by those prayers through my mother's story.

Our heritage is rich with faith stories that may touch our lives and empower us for living our faith in the midst of life's challenges. Look at your family tree. Try to learn the stories of individuals as far back as you can go. If you are adopted, don't let this daunt you. You have a choice of exploring the tree of your birth parents or affirming your adoptive parents' heritage as your own, much as we affirm our adoption into the family of God.

As you process these stories, you may want to examine the witness of other women and men who lived by faith throughout the history of Christianity. The uniqueness of the Christian community is that we are all part of a larger family, the family of God. And so our faith can grow as we learn the stories recorded in church history (including the early church) and as we read the professions of the faithful ones centuries before Christ. Isn't it wonderful to be a distinctive part of such a large family? You and I are like pieces in God's eternal puzzle, like brushstrokes on God's master canvas. We belong somewhere and to someone. Recognizing our uniqueness and that of our children within the larger framework of God's history brings a sense of integrity, worth, and wholeness to our lives. That's what our children will see in us.

How do our children contribute to our faith?

Our faith buds and grows when we hear and read stories of previous generations who lived by faith. It is more directly affected by our own growing-up experiences, particularly through the influences of and atmosphere in our parental home. Further bursting forth occurs through study, reading, reflection, worship, observation, and personal experience. We eagerly desire a maturing, growing faith we can communicate to the next generation. In the process, we may miss an opportunity for growth we had not considered, namely, in our children.

If God is at the center of existence and the ground of our being, and if all are created in the divine image empowered by God's breath of life (Genesis 2:7), we must believe that our children are spiritual beings. These young ones unconsciously bring God to us if we can but develop a spiritual sensitivity that touches our consciousness at many levels of awareness. If we allow our faith to permeate every aspect of our life, we begin to meet the Divine in the most amazing places and at the most amazing times. If we believe God speaks to us through our children, we are humbled by the miracle of such greatness being manifested through such innocence. Yet that's precisely what Jesus says (Matthew 21:16).

This spiritual being may speak to you through the marvel of birth, the wonder of adoption, the phenomenon of growth and change, the smiles, laughter, comments, and stories. This is the God-given spiritual dimension of your child coming to you and communicating with your inner spiritual self, bringing another aspect of God to your growing faith. Never underestimate the amazement of God working in and through your child. It will make all the difference to your faith and the way you perceive that young one beside you. Sharing faith then becomes two-sided: one side where you bring yourself and the other side where your child, this spiritual being, unconsciously contributes to your faith.

Travel tips

In this first chapter we have defined the meaning of faith and confronted ourselves with the nature of our personal commitment. We have become more aware of the faith influences of other generations, particularly the home in which we grew up. Being in touch with our own experiences and reflecting on them can make us more sensitive to how faith may be shared with our children. While you pack lunches and other supplies for the journey through the woods, reflect on some of the following:

- Parenting is a unique responsibility. Responsible parenting is more than a biological fact of life. It is a ministry to the whole child—physically, emotionally, intellectually, socially, and spiritually.
- Parenting requires the recognition that we do not own our child. These children have been entrusted to us. We need an openness that does not control or overpower.
- Parenting is a cooperative venture with God. Our children are not replicas of ourselves. They will make faith choices (even as we guide them) in ways unique to them. They're like rosebushes. We nurture, till, water, even provide light, but in the end they will bloom when they are ready, when they are touched by the hand of the Eternal Gardener.

For review and response

Recap

1. Too readily we confuse faith with religion. Religion can be taught; faith is lived.

2. The faith of our children begins with the ways they perceive and experience us.

3. The belief that God is personally interested in us affirms our self-worth, empowers our faith, and makes it possible for us to be loving, caring persons who are able to communicate our faith to the next generation.

4. Faith is an experience, a daily live meeting with God that makes a difference in how one lives, acts, and converses.

5. The home where you grew up and the caregivers in that home were the first shapers of your idea of God.

6. By being aware of how the faith of the previous generation influenced you, you will also have more insight about how your children may be reading you.

7. Our heritage is rich with faith stories that may touch our lives and empower us for living the faith in the midst of life's challenges.

8. If we believe God speaks to us through our children, we are humbled by the miracle of such greatness being manifested through such innocence.

9. Responsible parenting is more than a biological fact of life; it is a ministry to the whole child, a cooperative venture with God.

What then shall we do?

1. Evaluate the nature of your personal relationship with God and decide where you desire to grow and change.

2. Determine how your home environment influenced

your childhood faith development and assess what it is you want your children to see in you.

3. Collect faith stories from your family and church history. Allow divine transformation to take place in your life as you relive what those before you have experienced. Share these stories with your children.

For family

Family time

1. *Family night and family council.* Establish one evening a week as Family Night with all family members committed to being present. Make a special meal or order out. After the meal, have devotions together and then set up a Family Council, which all members take turns leading. Our council developed a formula that our five-year-old could use: "Family Council is now in session. Any hurts, worries, or concerns?" After the discussion came the next agenda item, "What do we want to do tonight?"

2. *Faith screen.* On a sheet of newsprint, draw a large computer monitor. Divide the screen into as many sections as you have family members. Suggest that each person draw a computer image illustrating how much God loves us. After each one shares their input, hang the Faith Screen in a visible area of the house. Note that this composite helps us remember God's love in different ways throughout the week.

3. *Snow party.* Have a winter snow party. Make a bonfire in a snowdrift and roast wieners. Serve hot cocoa. Make snow angels. Draw attention to the uniqueness of each angel just as we, God's creations, are unique.

4. *Park walk.* On a warm day, spend some time in the park. Take sandwiches and pop. Prepare a list of items for a nature scavenger hunt and play the game. When the collec-

tions are in, note the specialness of God's creation. Use a magnifying glass to focus on the intricacies of created things. Invite the children's comments by asking, "What does this say to you about God?"

5. *Country ride.* Take a car ride into the country. Play a game where each one tries to identify something God created. Stop for ice cream. Note that this is also part of God's creation: cream is from cows and sugar is from cane. Sing songs as you drive along. Here's one to the tune of "For God So Loved Us": "God made the sunshine, God made the moonlight, the starry skies and oceans blue. (Chorus) We thank-you, God, for all creation, and for the fun time we had today." Ask children for other words to substitute in the stanza based on things they saw along the way, or insert words like ice cream, sugar, creamy milk, vanilla, etc.

Celebrate the family

Celebrate the graduate. Let your children know they are God's special creation. Develop a "graduation" mentality where you celebrate the usual graduation events but also many firsts or lasts in your child's life, such as the beginning and end of each grade in church or school, the first paper route, first allowance, learning to tie a shoe, first book read or poem memorized, and so on. For a simple celebration, keep balloons on hand. On the special day, your child selects the menu, dessert, or treat, and someone presents the balloon. The rest of the family may write words or draw symbols on the balloon. Another option is to select a specific candleholder and candle to serve as a Graduate Candle, which is lit at mealtime for the graduate.

An idea for a family night activity

Explore your community. You may have lived in your community for years without realizing how much you can learn and experience only short distances from home. Visit parks, explore historic sites, or make appointments to visit people with unique professions or hobbies. Years ago our family visited a farmer whose pride was the many-colored breeds of pheasants he raised. Among other things, we cycled to an historic mill, explored old cemeteries, and flew kites. Use your imagination. Scan your local newspaper for ideas and information.

For study

Search the Scriptures

"While they [Joseph and Mary] were there, the time came for the baby to be born, and she gave birth to her first-born, a son" (Luke 2:6-7a).

1. Identify incidents in the opening chapters of Matthew and Luke that best illustrate the faith life of Mary and Joseph.

2. List the religious practices these new parents engaged in and reflect on how these practices may or may not have enhanced their faith life.

Discuss the questions

1. Respond to the statement: The faith of our children begins by the way they perceive and experience us.

2. Discuss: The home where you grew up and the care-givers in that home were the first shapers of your idea of God.

3. Which, or whose, faith stories have influenced your life?

Engage in group response

1. Draw a large family tree and name the branches after parents and other people who influenced your faith during

childhood. Share the stories behind three of the names on your tree with the group.

2. Write a letter to yourself on the topic "What my God-given faith means to me." Add a P.S. in which you list ways you want your children to understand what that faith means to you. If you wish, share your letter with the group.

3. Out of the materials you have looked at today, determine five values or experiences you would like to pass on to your children. Write them on slips of paper. Share these with each other. How many of these are similar? What are some ways you can support one another in trying to make these faith expressions real for your children?

Chapter 2

In a Grape Arbor

Reflections on Parents' Beliefs and What Those Beliefs Communicate to Children

....

Quiet moments before the journey

Lunch is packed and the children have come in from play. While they drink some juice before starting the journey, take a few moments in your quiet grape arbor to reflect. Arbors are wonderful places for solitude and brief escape. Vines grow rapidly and dark green leaves provide shade and shelter. Our grape arbor covers a wooden deck, providing privacy and a place for reflection. Some plant grapes around gazebos for a secluded spot to drink tea or to have a quiet conversation. For others the shaded leaves and refreshing clusters of grapes may be a state of mind, a visualized scene of escape where one can think, meditate, pray, and come away refreshed. All parents need a grape arbor, actual or in one's mind: a briefly closed door, moments to refuel and come away revitalized, better able to share faith with their children.

You have a few moments in this quiet place. Shut out the noises and give further thought to the meaning of your faith and how that faith is communicated to your children. We talked about how the faith of those who are a part of our spiritual and biological family tree encourages our faith. As our faith grows, it, in turn, is passed on to the next generation. What we did not discuss is the fact that the beliefs we hold about various aspects of our faith directly affect the nature of our faith and how that faith is relayed to our children in word, attitude, and deed. Out of many questions, I have selected several to help you weigh the pros and cons of how your beliefs do and will affect your faith.

Meditate prayerfully and thoughtfully on your beliefs—not for the purpose of being right or wrong. The questions raised in this chapter are not judgments. They give opportunity to think about what we believe and how that belief may affect our life and relationships. That doesn't mean we have all the answers. Even the wisest one among us understands little of the divine. The eternal world is far beyond our grasp and human comprehension (Isaiah 55:8-9). Faith is not faith if everything is spelled out and certain. Faith requires a deep, growing trust in a God who we believe is trustworthy. We need to pray for wisdom and insight as we continue to grow in faith, a faith we want to share with our children.

What do you believe about God?

We may affirm the God of the Bible and the God professed in the doctrines of our church or in the Apostles' Creed. We may affirm God as represented in a certain theology or way of thinking. But our life and relationships may be influenced by beliefs about God of which we are not even aware. Some beliefs may dominate our lives; others may creep in during times of crisis. Some aspects of the God in which we believe may reflect how we experienced our parents during our early formative years and the tidbits we learned in Sunday school taught by someone expressing an understanding of God based on his or her earlier perceptions.

In *Your God Is Too Small* (Phoenix Press, 1986) J. B. Phillips discussed views of God that can limit our growth and maturation in faith. For some, God is the creator, the almighty force who created us and then left us to fend for ourselves. Who has not experienced times of depression, of feeling alone with the cry of Jesus on the cross, "My God, my God, why have you forsaken me?" on his or her lips? This is a normal human response to crisis. But if a sense of isolation becomes an inner belief that God is always remote and distant, how does that affect our faith? What does that inner belief communicate to a child about God?

For some, God is a judge who watches and angrily lets us know how bad we are. We need reminders of wrongdoing so that we can confess our sin and ask forgiveness. But if we constantly feel guilty or live in fear of God's wrath—despite our professions that God is love—the God we really believe in may be a harsh taskmaster. Real guilt comes as a result of having done wrong. False guilt is like a persistent canker sore; you can't get rid of it because you can't do anything right. It is possible that in times of crisis we may catch ourselves thinking "What have I done to deserve this punishment?" That's a normal human response. But if we constantly feel guilty and live in fear of being punished, how does that affect our faith? What does that inner belief communicate to a child about God?

For some, God is a hypodermic needle, an injection at regular intervals to make us feel good when we need it. A woman once said to me, "I go to church because I need that shot in the arm to get me through the week." That's normal human response. The line between worship of the almighty God and getting what we want from God can become very thin. If we focus primarily on the latter, we may unconsciously think of God in terms of what our faith does for us— how our needs are met. We may pray only because it makes us feel good or because we need something. In our consumer-oriented society, we can easily become consumers of religion and unconsciously assume God to be at our beck and call like some favorite pet. Yet we know that a relationship in which one does all the taking and the other all the giving cannot grow. If our actions show that this is our inner belief, how will we share the meaning of prayer with our child? If deep down we believe it is God's job to make us happy and to make us feel good, what does this inner belief communicate to our child about God?

There are many other beliefs about God that unconsciously sneak into our faith lives. These mixtures may surprise us. That's why times of reflection may help us sift out the helpful and least helpful dimensions of our faith and life.

No one has a full understanding of God. What the greatest saint or theologian among us can know about God would fit on the head of a pin. Even God's people of the Old Testament demonstrated views that were not in keeping with God's original intent for humanity (see Genesis 1 and 2). More often they reflected the society in which they lived than the ways of God. Thus the same people who believed in an almighty, merciful, guiding God also believed in a God of war, punishment, and destruction.

Not having a full understanding of God doesn't mean we are in a hopeless situation. Rather, it shows what a great and marvelous God we have. It keeps us from trying to bring God down to our own level and warns us against trying to make God over into our image. It also reminds us that our faith lives can grow richer and fuller as we search for deeper understanding through study, prayer, and fellowship with other believers. Living two thousand years on this side of the resurrection gives us a great advantage in learning to know God. The Christian faith affirms that Jesus Christ, the incarnate son of God, was God among us. By becoming human and living in our midst, God lived as we live, felt as we feel, and spoke to us in words we can understand. Jesus called God *Abba* (Daddy), a God who loves the world enough to die for it. Jesus demonstrated a God of mercy and compassion, a God who calls us to committed discipleship. The incarnate God is a God who cares about each individual; a God who freely forgives; a God who accepts all people regardless of social standing, race, gender, or age; a God who loves all people—even the enemy. This God heals the broken-hearted, helps the suffering, and brings abundant life to all. This God plays no favorites: the rain falls on the just and on the unjust, and the sins of the past generations are not visited on the children. And this is only the beginning. The challenge for parents and people of faith is to study the Gospels and explore the meaning of Jesus' teachings as we try to answer the question "What do you believe about God?"

What do you believe about Jesus?

This seems like a simple question. "Everyone knows," we say, "that Jesus came to die for our sins so that we can go to heaven." But is that all? Or is there more?

According to the angel's message (Luke 2:11) the joyful news was not only the Savior's birth but also the advent of his lordship. Proclaiming Jesus as Savior can't be separated from accepting him as lord of one's life. To know Jesus as Savior and Lord is to recognize him as both crucified and resurrected. The empty cross symbolizes not only a Christ who died but also a Lord who cannot be contained by death. In 1 Corinthians 15 Paul maintains that Christ's resurrection is the focus of the gospel. Without it there is no good news. The good news is that a living Lord who died for us proclaims forgiveness, gives us the abundant life now (John 10:10) and hope for eternity. Our lives can be lived with meaning, joy, and anticipation. Do our children see that faith in us?

To know the resurrected Jesus as both Savior and Lord also means we are accountable for how we live in the here and now. Jesus proclaimed that God's reign is both present and future (Matthew 13:31-53, 25:1-46). Jesus exemplified the meaning of the Christian life through his ministry, teachings, and mission (Matthew 5–7, Luke 4:18-19). Believers are to reflect Christ in conduct, ethics, morality, and motive. Too easily we flow with the stream and become mirrors of society. The trademark of the Christian is Jesus' Great Commandment: "'Love the Lord your God with all your heart and with all your soul and with all your mind.' This is the first and greatest commandment. And the second is like it: 'Love your neighbor as yourself'" (Matthew 22:37-39). How does our daily life—all that we do and say—express this kind of faith to our children? As we share our faith with our children, what does it mean when we say "Jesus Christ is my Savior and Lord of my life"?

What do you believe about the Holy Spirit?

A number of years ago while writing curriculum on the book of Acts, I became aware of how little I knew about the Holy Spirit. Rarely had I heard a sermon on the subject, and the ones I did hear spoke of a spiritual, elusive being. Hymns I studied focused on gentle, dovelike qualities of a rather benign being. I studied Acts 1:8, "You will receive power," and woke up. The word for power in Greek is dunamais, the root of our word dynamite. The Holy Spirit is the empowering force of God. The Holy Spirit makes it possible to be Christian in a courageous, unswerving way. A short time later I wrote the hymn "Holy Spirit, Come with Power." (See *Hymnal: A Worship Book,* Faith & Life Press, Brethren Press, and Mennonite Publishing House, 1992, for a setting of this hymn.)

What do you believe about the Holy Spirit and how does that belief affect your life? Is the Spirit only a one-time phenomenon described in Acts 2? Is the Spirit a feeling? Is the Spirit an ecstatic means of coping when one comes to the end of one's rope? Or is there more?

If the Holy Spirit is God, that Spirit can't be relegated to first-century Pentecost. The Spirit of God appears in Genesis 1:2, hovering, waiting to empower created humanity. In the Old Testament, individuals engaged in a specific task occasionally experienced the Spirit's power. In the Gospels, the Spirit is mentioned several times in reference to events in Jesus' life (Matthew 3:16, 4:1, Mark 1:8). Jesus taught his followers that the Holy Spirit would come to them as a counselor, the spirit of truth, and as a promised gift. They would know the Holy Spirit as presence, teacher, reminder, guide, one who convicts, one who gives power (John 14:16-17, 26, 16:7-15, Acts 1:4-8). After Christ's ascension, the gathered believers experienced the full impact of the Holy Spirit at Pentecost. The book of Acts tells us how fear and cowardice were replaced by a joy and courage that set the world on fire. Though that enthusiasm gradually faded, the Spirit was never crucified, only tamed. At Corinth, where there was a divisive church, many believers focused on the Holy Spirit primarily as personal ecstasy and speaking in tongues (*glossolalia*). When some insisted that speaking in tongues was the most important gift, others felt left out. Belief in the Spirit had become a hurting rather than a healing force. What happened to the power?

Christians today continue to think about the Holy Spirit in different ways. Rather than emphasizing only one part of the Holy Spirit's activity, look at the broader understanding taught by Jesus. Then reflect on your own beliefs. What difference does the Holy Spirit make in our lives? If our child loses an argument with a peer and wants to get even, can we share faith in a power that can help us live above pettiness? Or if an older child faces a difficult decision, can we lead her in prayer that assures her that the Counselor will guide, teach, and give her the wisdom to make the best choice?

What do you believe about the triune God?

Do you ever think of God as the Trinity? By doing so, we fit our beliefs about God, about Jesus, and about the Holy Spirit into one larger picture. The word Trinity is not in the Bible, but the concept is. Genesis 1 refers to God as plural, and Jesus speaks of God as Father, Son, and Holy Spirit in Matthew 28:19. Early theologians conceived the term Trinity to help identify the many aspects of God and the mysterious ways in which this divinity continues to be self-revealing. We experience God as Creator and Sustainer, the Redeeming Lord, and the Empowering One—Father (parent), Son, and Holy Spirit.

Our minds can't really grasp the meaning of the Trinity. Three in one and one in three is a mystery that confesses how little we know about God. One could say that the Trinity is more like the three-leaved shamrock than three separate plants. But there is much more to it than that. With our limited awareness, belief in a triune God helps us understand how it is possible for God to be far away yet near, beyond our comprehension yet communicating with us, everywhere yet living within us. It keeps us from thinking of God in only one certain way.

Why is it important to reflect on the Trinity as we share our faith with our children?

If we isolate God the parent from Christ and Spirit and focus on the greatness and glory of the Creator, we are left without a message of redemption and empowerment. If we glory only in the Creator, what can we share with our child about power and presence when he feels down or is having problems? about forgiveness when she's done wrong?

If we separate Jesus the redeeming Lord from God and Spirit and focus solely on salvation and forgiveness, we may ignore the greatness and mystery of God. We may close ourselves to seeing the many ways God may bring us and our children to faith. If we glory only in the Savior, how will we share a faith that embodies the Spirit's power, vision, and mission?

If we sequester the Holy Spirit away from an understanding of God's great plan for humanity (Ephesians 1) or the redemptive act of Jesus Christ and his call to discipleship, the power needed for mission and outreach may become peripheral. We may think of our religious experience as mainly emotional and personal. If we glory only in the Spirit, how will we share a faith that speaks of forgiveness, outreach, and the greatness of the everlasting God?

Even as we focus on the Trinity, we must realize that God can't be put into a niche. We humans want to do just that. We lean toward an understanding of God that feels comfortable to us, one that meets our needs. God is much more than the Trinity or an individual member of it. We need to acknowledge our limited ability to perceive divinity.

Whether God is plural or many aspects of one, we can't know. Our brains are too small. But to grow in faith, we need to incorporate as much about God as we can grasp and experience and never confine God to one limited view. The great God, the triune God, is the greatest Christmas present ever given to humanity—but the divine cannot be boxed, wrapped, or ribboned. The moment we confine God, we become our own God, because we assume we're capable of defining and limiting God.

What is our understanding of the triune God? How does that affect our faith, that center of our lives, with our children?

What does it mean to be human?

When you look at another person, younger or older, what do you see? Whom do you see? According to Genesis 2, the human is different from all the rest of creation. The human is endowed with the breath of God. A Jewish theologian maintains that our violent, brutal world—focused on a mechanistic, dispensable view of persons—has replaced the basic understanding that the human is a sacred being. To many, life is cheap. For others, quality of life is the right of a privileged few. What does that say about the human as sacred?

The other person, no matter whom he or she is, is created in the image of God. Sometimes this is hard to remember, not only because of our biases but also because of whom the other person is. If we treat anyone as less than sacred, we are saying that that person isn't human. Viewing the other as sacred leaves no room for physical, emotional, or psychological abuse that destroys and abases, that preys on the weak and helpless. Our superior size and ability never justifies treating our children as less than sacred beings.

We live in an age of violence. Nearly every evening we hear about at least one murder or other form of violence on the news. Many urban families live in fear. Recently a newspaper reported on the decreased popularity of sandlot baseball because it's not safe for children to be away from adult supervision. Now they play baseball in cul-de-sacs with parents nearby.

There are many other ways at home and in church that the sacredness of an individual is disregarded: pettiness, uncontrolled anger, put-downs, destructive criticism. Treating our children with respect is one of the greatest gifts we can give to them. Respect is a way of sharing faith in a God who created us sacred, regardless of status or age.

Sacredness of the other is central to both Jewish and Christian faith. Jesus met young and old, male and female, rich and poor, prostitutes, the ill—all strata of society—with respect and compassion. We sometimes lack that ability. Using tunnel vision, we can focus on one aspect of sacredness. We may put all our eggs in the basket of a peace position that is antiwar or against capital punishment or strongly antiabortion. By focusing narrowly, someone supporting a peace stance may refuse to go to war yet tolerate violence in the home. Someone against capital punishment may have little concern about making social changes that would give young people in bad situations a better chance in life. Someone who is strongly antiabortion may justify using any means to accomplish that end but may not care about the unwanted, abandoned children in our society. The biblical view of the human as sacred takes the whole of a person's life into consideration. Sacredness involves not only life and death issues in certain narrow areas but also the quality of life we are willing to help others attain.

How broad or narrow is your view of human sacredness? How does it affect the way you share your faith with young ones? If a child knows her parents advocate for peace but they also angrily slap her face, what will she learn about faith? If a child sees a newspaper picture of a protester carrying a sign that says "Death to gays!" how will we respond?

One cannot address the question of sacredness without discussing sin. Do you see children as born sinners? Are children born innocent and good—a gift of God's grace—and only later become sinners? Are infants spiritual beings—does even a young baby have something of God within? Are babies moral beings with the potential to choose good or bad based on emotional and psychological development, beings who may eventually make a well-reasoned commitment to follow Jesus Christ?

People disagree on the answers to these questions. Our answers give some clues to what we believe about the sacredness of children. All views have their pros and cons. If we believe a child is born a sinner, we may be concerned about infant baptism. Or we may propel our child toward an early experience of salvation. If we believe children are born as spiritual beings, we may appreciate their sacredness but neglect to nurture faith, assuming God is at work in the child. If we believe children are born as innocent or moral beings with the potential for choosing good or evil, we will want to understnad how faith develops in children and how it relates to moral and emotional development. If we believe children become morally accountable in adolescence, we may look ahead to that time rather than focusing on the process of faith nurture and faith sharing in younger children.

What do you believe about the meaning of being human? about the sacredness of the other? about being created in the image of God? How do your views of sin and grace affect the way you share your personal faith with your child?

What do you believe about prayer?

I once heard a sermon based on the hymn "Prayer Is the Soul's Sincere Desire." The minister stressed that the words we speak may not be our actual prayer. Our prayers are the thoughts, feelings, moods, wants, and wishes deep inside us. What is prayer? What governs our prayer life? What do we believe about prayer? What does prayer have to do with faith? Is prayer something to do, or is it a state of being? Is prayer something to do in a state of being?

This chapter focused on our spoken or unspoken

beliefs about the divine and humanity. We conclude by looking at our spoken or unspoken beliefs about prayer. How are these subjects related? What we believe about the Trinity— God, Jesus, and the Holy Spirit—and what it means to be human affect how we perceive and experience prayer.

Prayer links us to God. It connects what we believe about God with what we believe about ourselves and forms a basis for communication. Prayer defines the nature of our relationship to God. Jesus gave us the Lord's Prayer (Matthew 6:9-13) as a model for prayer. This prayer can guide our thinking and help keep our communication with God from becoming one-sided. It begins with praise of the great, holy God and a commitment to God's will. The Lord's Prayer requests the meeting of physical needs, healing of relationships, and wisdom for making positive decisions. It recognizes God's power and glory as the source for true kingdom living, now and forever.

In Matthew 6:5 Jesus emphasized that prayer is a relationship, not a public demonstration. In Matthew 7:7-12 Jesus again spoke of prayer as a relationship that requires persistence. At the same time he noted that God, even more than a parent, gives only good gifts.

Jesus made other references to prayer. He prayed in the presence of others (John 11:41-42, 17:1) and often retreated to the mountains to pray. His prayer of agony on the Mount of Olives (Luke 22:39-46) preceded his arrest and crucifixion. His last words were a prayer of intercession, "Father, forgive them, for they do not know what they are doing," followed by "Father, into your hands I commit my spirit" (Luke 23:34,46). Prayer was at the heart of everything Jesus did and said. It grew out of and reflected his relationship with God.

Prayer is communication between God and humanity. But the nature of that communication depends on us. We can give lip service and say all the right words, but if our hearts aren't in it, we can merely say, "We have prayed." At other times we may not be able to pray at all. At those difficult times when no words come, a memorized psalm, a hymn, or a prayerbook can become our guide. Often these hard times are followed by a spurt of growth and renewal. We know we will pray again because without prayer there is no real communication.

Prayer is both words and a state of being—it is a relationship. We can't describe all the dynamics of prayer any more than we can describe the ebb and flow of any significant relationship. Prayer is praise, adoration, petition, intercession, confession. Above all, prayer is listening. God wants the opportunity to speak, to instruct, to guide. God's voice comes to us in many different ways and at most unexpected times. It takes energy, time, and awareness to develop the listening skills needed to hear God's voice.

There are many aspects to prayer. For some, prayer is mostly praise and intercession. For some, prayer is mainly asking—trying to get what we want, or praying for a good feeling inside. We may think that God will bless us if we remember to pray every day. Or we may feel that we need to pray to avert dangers or God's displeasure. Early influences from home and childhood may guide our prayer life. How do our prayers compare with the model Jesus gave us in Matthew 6:9?

We can test out the nature of our prayers through an understanding of everyday life. How would a relationship with a spouse or close friend work if we did all the talking, all the asking, none of the listening, and rarely gave praise or affirmation? How often are our prayers like this? A growing relationship requires mutuality; both parties need to speak and listen.

The promise of a rich prayer life requires the same dynamics as our human relationships. But there the metaphor ends. Communicating with God demands much more of us than any human relationship. Worship, praise, and adoration are requirements for our prayers because we are not dealing with an equal. We are not God's buddies. We are God's grateful servants. God, through Jesus Christ, has made it possible to attain a prayer relationship in which we may communicate personally with the creator of the universe, the redeemer of the world, and the empowering force of the church (Ephesians 1:3-23).

We do well to teach and model the importance of prayer to and for our children. I remember seeing my parents kneeling at their bedside in prayer. Seeing one's parents in prayer leaves a strong impression on a child. It gives the young one a sense of assurance: if mother and father are praying, all is well.

If we believe in the power of prayer, we can help our children attain an awareness of God. We may already involve children in ritual prayers at meals and bedtime. But a relationship can't be programmed. We must make room for spontaneity. When your child is sad, pray together. When your child is glad, praise God together. When your child is frightened, pray for comfort. When your child is worried, pray for wisdom. Help your children believe that God answers all prayers—not always as we want but in a way that is best. God sees the big picture; we don't.

Let your prayer life be a model for your child. Pray in your child's presence and let your prayers speak praise, thanks, intercession, request, confession. As your child learns to pray and becomes more aware of God's presence, your own faith may grow as you hear the simple, trusting words of your child's prayers. And as your faith grows and you continue to share it, your child learns more about God.

Travel tips

It's time to go. The issues raised are but a few of many that shape your faith as you think and respond to the questions you ask. Sometimes we may not even be aware that the questions we ask are deeply religious and related to the nature of our faith. We may talk about coping, stress, anxiety, depression, illness, family problems, and so on. But underneath flows a deeper current. It asks, "What is the meaning of life? What are my concerns about death? suffering? why me? why our family? Why does God allow evil to happen? Why do humans have the capacity for laughter and joy? What does it mean to exercise my free will? What does it mean to be Christian in the workplace? at home?" and many more.

It is important that you get to the root of your real feelings and identify your fears, hopes, longings, and concerns. Being honest with your feelings, rather than just repeating something you've been taught, leads to a genuine faith that comes out of your personal struggle and experience. Your children will respect the honesty and integrity with which you express a faith that has become real to you.

Being Christian and learning to share your unique faith is a *becoming* process. Your children will benefit and grow in an atmosphere where questions are asked, where new understandings are incorporated, where an open-mindedness allows all of you to think through the significance of a faith that germinates and sprouts, developing from a seedling into a tall bush (Mark 4:30-32). As you leave the yard, here are further things to think about.

1. The story *Jonathan Livingston Seagull,* by Richard Bach, tells of a gull who must decide whether to spend life grubbing for food, squabbling, and fighting off predators, or whether to fly to ever more dizzying heights toward the glory

of the sun. This is a decision you as a Christian must make. We may make a decision to follow Jesus Christ and participate in the expected church activities and that's it. We may get so caught up with the daily grind, overwhelmed by parental responsibilities, that our wings feel clipped and we no longer fly towards the ever fuller glory of the Son. The greatest favor we can do our children in communicating our faith is to decide on our life priority, to open our minds to God in new ways, to share ways we have experienced God in our day, and to allow this joyous atmosphere to permeate our home.

2. Your faith experience is not separate from who you are. It is the core of your being, the center of your existence, and it changes attitudes, motives, relationships, and ways of thinking. Like salt, it brings flavor to everything you do and say. Like light, it exposes new insights, values, and hope to those touched by its rays (Matthew 5:13-16). Becoming more Christian is a metamorphosis from imprisonment in a cocoon to the freedom and grace of a winged creature. It is grounded in having the mind of Christ; our thought patterns and habits determine our behavior, evidenced by how we share faith and life with our children (Romans 12:1-2, 1 Corinthians 2:16b).

For review and response

Recap

1. The beliefs we hold about various aspects of our faith directly affect the nature of our faith and how that faith is relayed to our children in word, attitude, and deed.

2. Unless we've been growing, studying, and reflecting, the God we have may be a reflection of how we perceived our parents during our early formative years and the tidbits we learned in Sunday school.

3. The closest we can come to knowing God is

through the incarnate Jesus Christ who came to show us what God is like.

4. The Holy Spirit is the empowering force of God. The Holy Spirit makes it possible to be Christian in a courageous, unswerving way.

5. God is much more than the Trinity or an individual member of it, and we need to acknowledge our limited ability to perceive divinity.

6. Viewing another person as sacred leaves no room for physical, emotional, or psychological abuse that destroys and abases, that preys on the weak and helpless.

7. Sacredness involves not only life-and-death issues in certain narrow areas but also the quality of life we are willing to help others attain.

8. Prayer defines the nature of our relationship to God.

What then shall we do?

1. Don't confuse questioning with doubt and don't confuse doubt with lack of faith. Faith is a risk we take; it can't be proven or it is no longer faith. Belief in the existence of God and faith in our resurrected Lord is the foundation on which all else is built. Without that, Christianity is futile (1 Corinthians 15:14). Growth is rooted in that initial risk. Some Christians see questions and doubts as a negative factor, not a normal incentive that spurs one to growth. Don't substitute the uneasiness and disquietude of your psalmist-type questions with simplistic answers that make you feel safe and secure. Trust God who loves you and allow the Spirit to open up new, untraveled vistas for you.

2. Allow God to build your faith by a process of searching. In a journal write down your questions and reflect on them as you drive to work or work at home. Talk about them with a friend, spouse, or group. When your family attends

worship, reflect on the readings in your bulletin or the words of a hymn. How do these thoughts broaden or restrict your understanding of the divine? What does that have to do with your questions? What does it mean for your daily life? Acknowledge that the Christian life is not a state of having achieved but of searching and growth (Philippians 3:12-14).

For family

Family time

1. *"God is ..." panel.* Fold a sheet of construction paper in half lengthwise and in large letters print the words *GOD IS...* on it. Cut ten feet of yarn. Thread the yarn through the bottom and top of the sheet and back again on the other side, providing a hanger at the top and leaving long lengths hanging down on either side. Cut five two-inch strips from another sheet of construction paper (more from a third sheet if needed). Each family member writes one word on a strip to describe God (for example, "love," "forgiving," etc.). Thread the yarn through each one, leaving about two inches between strips. Knot the yarn at the bottom. Hang it on the wall and talk about the many ways your family experiences God.

2. *Thank-you rocks.* Collect rocks and spray them with a clear, acrylic finish. With bright nail polish, paint the words THANK-YOU, GOD, FOR on each one. Talk about God's goodness and have each one add one word on his or her rock denoting something for which they are thankful. Read Psalm 95:1-7.

3. *Praise God.* Read Psalm 148:1-13. Note how all created beings praise God. Select created beings from the psalm and ask, "How would a _____ praise the Lord? (Example: sea creature. Let them use their imagination and have fun with this). Divide your family (or extended family) into two teams. On paper, each team tries to discover and list created things and

beings that members see indoors or outdoors (or tear pictures from magazines.) Share your findings. Compare the psalmist's words with your lists. If you found something not listed by the psalmist, say: "_____ praises God." Close with a short prayer where each member says: "I, (name), praise you for. ...."

4. *The healer.* Jesus helped and healed people. We help with healing when we show someone we care. Make or buy some gifts. Wrap and number them. Visit someone who is sick or elderly. Give the gifts and suggest that he or she open one of them each day in the numbered order. Sing some songs or tell some funny stories. Music and laughter are healing gifts that God has given us.

5. *Sing a Psalm.* Psalm 147:1 states that it is good to sing praises. Model an attitude of gratitude and praise for your children. Learn and sing the simple song "Praise the Lord." Sing it often as a table grace, while you work, play, or walk together.

Celebrate the family

Celebrate a hallowed evening. Halloween originally was a pagan Celtic festival celebrating the annual return of the spirits for winter hibernation. Missionaries following the Roman invasion of England and Scotland reshaped it into a religious holiday commemorating the saints of the church. They called it Hallowed Evening. Celebrate Hallowed Evening by showing pictures and talking about grandparents or others who have died. Share their stories of faith and life. If a relative is buried nearby, you may want to visit the cemetery during the day and talk about spiritual contributions of this person.

Another source says that Halloween also has its origin in a harvest festival. Those who had a bountiful crop were to give to those who did not. Stinginess resulted in public shame. This custom is the source of "trick or treat." Why not get back to the original custom and contact friends or church

Praise the Lord
(Psalm 147:1)

Words and Music by Anne N. Rupp

Allegretto (M.M. ♩ =104)

Praise the Lord! Praise   the   Lord!   Praise   the   Lord!   Praise   the   Lord
(Leader)   (Response)   (Leader)   (Response)

Praise the Lord! Praise   the Lord!   It   is   good to give prais - es   to   our God.
(Leader)   (Response)   (Leader)

(Group 1) Praise God.

To our   God.   Praise   the   Lord!   Praise   the   Lord!   Praise   God.
(Response)   (Leader)   (Response)   (Group 2)

members in advance? Go to these homes and collect items for a local food pantry. What other ways could you celebrate Halloween by giving, not getting?

An idea for a family night activity

Friendship tablecloth. Buy a large tablecloth and invite single friends or families for family night. (Try to include other cultures and races.) After the meal, clear the dishes and ask guests to write their names on the tablecloth. Someone in the family embroiders these names. Continue to invite old or new friends and see how many names your family accumulates. At a specified time, use your Family Night to thank God for these friends.

For study

Search the Scriptures

"Exalted to the right hand of God, he [Jesus] has received from the Father the promised Holy Spirit and has poured out what you now see and hear" (Acts 2:33).

In Peter's Pentecost sermon, he attributes their experience to members of the Trinity. How is each engaged?

In your own words, describe the work of God in Acts 1–2. How is the believer's experience different from or similar to your own?

Discuss the questions

1. What does the thought "Live a God-centered life" mean to you? How are your values, concerns, and relationships affected by that thought?

2. Look at the six subjects introduced in this chapter and discuss what you believe about each one. Test your beliefs

with one another. Discuss how your beliefs affect the way you share your faith with your children.

Engage in group response

1. Place a basket in the middle of the group. On slips of paper write down main beliefs you would like to pass on to your children. Drop your slips into the basket. One person reads them to the group. Share and discuss.

2. Each person draws a shield and divides it into six parts. In each section write a one- or two-word response to the six areas discussed, beginning with "God is like ...." Look at the whole shield and evaluate how integrated your faith is. Explain how your understanding affects the faith you share.

3. Shape a square of foil to depict a new way God has recently been revealed to you through thought or experience. Share with the group.

Chapter 3

The Virgin Grasses

Emotional, Spiritual, and Moral Development of Children in the First Year

....

The journey begins

Y̲ou are on your way, children in hand (perhaps carrying an infant), walking down the narrow lane that leads to the woods. A soft breeze steals toward you from the distant green, wisps of spring on its breath. The warm sun plays peek-a-boo with the woolly clouds that cluster around it and your eldest points out their shapes as they shift across the sky. It is a beautiful day for your journey. Before you enter the woods, look around you. Someone burned the open fields last fall, and wherever you look you now see green shoots bursting from the soil. Drinking up the sunlight and basking in the rain, these virgin grasses radiate the newness of life. Some are longer, some shorter and thicker, but they all have one thing in common—they are beginners. They will change, grow, and become something quite different than they are now, and should you travel this way again, you would hardly recognize them.

These virgin grasses are not unlike our beginning and the beginnings of our children. The journey with our children is never static. It is filled with vibrant growth and vitality. At the same time the child is growing in size and ability, that young one is also growing emotionally, intellectually, spiritually, and morally. We need to understand this development *as one whole* because that's how God made us. We cannot minister only to spiritual needs and ignore the child's emotional needs. Nor can we minister only to a child's physical needs and ignore moral development. To do so is to create an imbalance that forces starvation in some aspect of the child's development. How then do we communicate faith to our children (and in this chapter particularly our very young children) in the midst of all this well-ordered transformation?

Before you continue your quiet walk through these virgin grasses, ask yourself several questions.

What must it be like to be little?

During my years as a children's editor, a writer submitted an article called "Get Down on Your Knees." I expected an article describing the need to pray for our children. Praying for our children is one of the most important things we can do. But prayer wasn't the writer's focus. She was talking about size. "What must it be like to see the world and those towering humans around us from this miniature height? Get on your knees and find out," was her theme.

Have you ever thought what it must be like to be an infant? You won't remember being squeezed and pushed through the birth canal into alien territory or how your screams, cries, or whimpers became the only effective way to initially establish territorial rights. There you lay, totally dependent on these giants leaning over you, reinforcing the fact that you were indeed the center of their universe. You cried and they came running. They held you, burped you, cuddled you, and made you feel welcome on earth. That's how it should be and that's how it is for your newborn.

Your baby's life holds several foci—moving from one breast to the other, one bottle to the other, wet bottom to dry bottom, out of crib or cradle into comforting arms. That's the way it should be. But being that little has its limitations. Your infant spends her small life looking at feet and ankles until someone picks her up and The Face appears. At that point she begins to identify feeling with face.

But it isn't long before the roots under these little virgin grasses urge them to grow, change, smile, laugh, and respond. There's nothing static about being a baby. During the first year of life, babies go through more changes and transformations than at any other time of life, and parents need to adjust and encourage accordingly.

I kept a daily diary of our son from infancy to age two and was amazed at all the "firsts" that occurred during the first twelve months. Suddenly the body says "crawl!" The tooth says "I'm coming." The mind says "stand" and the feet say "walk." By the time they reach one year of age, they may wriggle away when held, yet always come back to the one who holds and provides. No matter how many feet they see, they know that this caregiving giant can be depended on.

But these changes may also knock parents for a loop. They no longer have 100 percent control. As infants move from total dependence toward toddlerhood, parents must learn to encourage the child's progress, not discourage it. These little ones don't know right from wrong. They are in a stage of innocence, God's gift to them and you. As they move from total dependence, their world gets larger and they begin to try it on, much as we try on a new dress or suit. This is another of God's gifts.

The stamina required of a parent nurturing an infant and growing baby defies description. After you've been up for night feedings, ear infections, or whatever may come your way, you may be so groggy and tired that you don't have the energy to love and nurture your child as you would wish. A young mother said to me, "I'm not getting my sleep and I'm tired all the time. When I'm tired I get depressed." Don't nurse your guilt. This time will soon pass, so take all the cat-naps you can, prioritize the care of your baby, and rely on God to sustain and empower you. Several months later the same mother said, "Things are looking a lot better."

Even as you nurture and love, remember you don't own this child. Your baby has been entrusted to you. Perhaps all children should be called Grace, which implies a free gift from God.

Can this parent be trusted?

The first year is the most critical year of one's whole life. It undergirds all faith experience. During this first year, when much physical change and growth take place, the basis for emotional, intellectual, spiritual, and moral development is embedded in the child-caregiver relationship.

During these early months, the child will either learn to *trust* (the basis for emotional development and the foundation of faith) or *distrust*. If the child learns that the adult world is trustworthy, further positive emotional and spiritual development can occur. If the infant doesn't learn to trust the caregiver, trust will be usurped by distrust. How the infant and young child experience the caregiving parent is directly related to how that youngster will perceive God.

Some time ago I viewed a film about children in an orphanage who had not been held or nurtured. Some at age two were unable to walk. One-year-olds couldn't sit or talk and resisted being held. They couldn't trust. It took much patience to nurture and encourage these young children, but gradually their physical and relational skills developed.

I counseled a sixteen-year-old who told me she repeatedly hit her nine-month-old baby on the hands with a ruler. "I'm teaching her to mind," she said. She herself had been physically abused at home. This was all she knew. At age sixteen she was depressed and suicidal. What was her baby learning about trust? If a caregiver is one who keeps hitting you for reasons you can't understand, how will this child perceive God as dependable and loving later on?

In our day we are constantly reading about the physical and sexual abuse of babies. There are many other ways of creating distrust: emotional abuse, withholding nurture and love, punitive voice and behavior, abandonment (physical or emotional), and undependability, to name but a few. These destroy the infant's trust (the foundation of faith) and can create a person who later finds the world undependable, depressing, and even meaningless.

Is it okay to be a less-than-perfect parent?

A word of caution: We will never have perfect trust nor will we be able to give that whole gift to our child. But being aware of our task can help us be more conscious of our infant's needs and more intentional in seeking ways to build trust.

None of us are perfect parents. Those who think they are may be out of touch with their feelings. Like perfectionists I've known, they may be rigid and demanding. I knew a woman who considered herself the perfect mother and her first son conformed to her standards. Long, dark curls, gentle care of toys and faultless behavior all affirmed her belief that she knew how to raise the perfect child. She looked askance at children who didn't measure up and wouldn't allow her son to play with some of them. When her second son was born, something changed. This young one played in the mud, broke the toys, evaded her rules, and always seemed to be dirty. The perfect mother soon learned about her limitations and eventually realized that early childhood is growth and spontaneity, not conformity to a mold. When the third baby arrived, she was much more flexible.

This illustration can help us understand what parenting is about. When Scripture talks about "perfect," it is not referring to a morally faultless life. Jesus says, "Be perfect, therefore, as your heavenly Father is perfect" (Matthew 5:48). This is spoken in the Sermon on the Mount in the context of relationships and the challenge to love one's enemies. God is love, and perfect love drives out fear (1 John 4:16, 18). Fear is the monster that cripples and freezes the potential of one's growth. We are to grow in love, to become more like Jesus (God) every day and allow our relationships, responses, and behaviors to flow out of that love. It's an ongoing process. Paul best expresses it in Philippians 3:12: "Not that I have already obtained all this, or have already been made perfect, but I press on to take hold of that for which Christ Jesus took hold of me."

I'm not making excuses for some of the poor parental decisions we make, or the days we feel less than loving. Rather, it's a reminder for us to grow, admit our mistakes, ask forgiveness, and realize how much we depend on the wisdom and counsel of the Holy Spirit through Jesus Christ. Sometimes, as we reflect on our mistakes, harsh words spoken, or days when we just didn't have the energy to invest ourselves in child rearing, we may wish we could do it over again. But the fact is, if we had a second chance, we'd make other errors. This recognition keeps us humble. Much of what happens in parenting is sheer grace.

When things get too tough, don't be embarrassed to ask for help. Don't give in to isolation and frustration. Remember, no one parent can be all things to a child. Be honest with yourself. Your honesty will help you be a better parent.

Here are some practical guidelines:

- Assess your strengths and limitations. Unless you are a single parent, make sure both spouses are involved and invested. Determine where you need family or extended family. When our son was an infant, I felt inadequate about medical questions. Thankfully, I had a good friend who was a nurse whom I could call on at any time. I didn't have to pretend with her.

- Evaluate feelings you may be struggling with. Are you angry about the demands? Do you feel trapped? inadequate? Remember, some parents are better with older children than with babies, and vice versa, but that doesn't mean you can't do a good job. Your love and faith are the foundation for all nurture, and your little one will feel that.

- Foster your spiritual growth and personal life. Make Psalm 23 your basic guidebook. When stressed, call in the troops. Find someone to talk to, someone who may lend a hand or even someone who will take over for a few hours while you leave the house. If you have a job or are invested in a career, you may come home exhausted. Make a transition as you drive home: sing, pray, meditate, scream, shout, take deep breaths, stop for coffee for five minutes in the park or whatever it takes to relax you. Take care of yourself spiritually and emotionally and you will be a more loving parent. If you can learn to shepherd your infant as does the Great Shepherd, you will indeed become a nurturing, trustworthy mother or father. I said become because parents don't just happen; they are made.

What does faith have to do with my child's spirituality?

We can interchange the words "sharing our faith" and "spiritual nurture," but our awareness is raised to another level when we add the term "our child's spirituality." Why? A child's faith is rooted in the ability to trust his or her parents, and that trust is the basis for a child's early experience of God. From this can grow a Christian faith that develops with further experience, understanding, nurture, and relationships. Think of it this way: A child growing up alone in the forest cannot know God as historically defined and experienced because faith is caught; it needs outside influences and relationships.

But the *spirituality* of a child is different and distinct. It is the innate sacredness of every infant born, God's divine breath that makes the human different from all other living things. We don't know how an innocent babe experiences God because infants don't have the capacity to identify or communicate spiritual reality. But the awareness of our child as a spiritual being makes ours a sacred trust; we dare not violate or abuse that trust. To do so is to tamper with holiness.

Travel tips

Let's continue our walk through the grasses. By now you are quite aware of these virgin surroundings with the fresh, green shoots pushing out of the ground, faces lifted to the sun. As you tread quietly along the path, I will walk with you for a while. We'll talk about the Everlasting Son, Jesus Christ, whose loving light you want to share with your little one from the very moment of birth. Here are a few things to remember:

1. You share your faith by building trust.

- To build trust, the child needs to perceive you as trustworthy. When you have to leave for a short time, jubilantly greet your child when you return. Let the baby know you're glad to see her and feed her growing awareness that you can be depended on to come back.
- To build trust, be available. Babies cry because they have a need, whether for diaper change, tummy ache, or you. Adults have a hard time saying, "Please hold me." Infants don't. If our faith professes that God is trustworthy, isn't this what we want to share about God with our infant?
- To build trust, we need to nurture the relationship. Your infant has both physical and relational needs. It is critical that he be held gently and warmly, rocked, and sung to. Be as kind as God is with you.

2. You share your faith by assuming the bonding is two-sided. In a recent radio interview, the guest noted that the communication between caregiver and baby is astounding. Studies showed that the mother could tell the infant's needs by the way the child was crying. If bonding is this intense, isn't it possible that something other than physical or relational needs can be communicated? In Japan, a music method asks parents to play a Bach recording daily from birth, assuming that artistry is being communicated to the child. Put that into the perspective of faith sharing.

- Play music for and sing hymns or songs to your infant.
- Keep eye contact and assure your baby that God loves her just as Mommy and Daddy do.
- Sit outdoors with your baby in the evening; show and tell her about the beautiful star world created by God.
- Let him touch the softness of the family pet. Tell him that God made Tiger or Rover.
- Laugh with your child. Laughter is an important God-given ingredient of faith.

• Recite Psalm 23. Pray with your infant.

This kind of communication may sound far-fetched, but we don't know what may communicate. This new earth guest may not understand the words but will feel the comfort and sincerity of voice and cradled arms.

3. You share your faith by getting used to sharing it. Sharing our faith does as much for the parent as for the child. Note the steps Jesus' parents took to incorporate their son into their faith traditions. What are some of the steps you would want to take in your home or local congregation?

Spiritual development is one part of a whole and begins at birth as do emotional, intellectual, moral, and physical development. If you begin at the beginning, God talk becomes as natural to you as other areas of growth. Some parents wait, taking care of all other areas of change and find themselves tongue-tied when they want to incorporate religious or faith elements. They expect the church to fill in the gaps. Important as formal Christian education is, it can't replace spiritual nurture by parents. If parents get used to sharing faith as an integral part of the infant's development, they won't feel like bears in the china closet when their little one turns two or three.

For review and response

Recap

1. The journey with our children is never static; it is filled with vibrant growth and development.

2. We cannot minister only to spiritual needs and ignore the child's emotional needs. Nor can we minister only to a child's physical needs and ignore moral development. To do so is to create an imbalance that forces starvation in some

aspect of the child's development.

3. As infants move from total dependence toward toddlerhood, parents must learn to encourage the child's progress, not discourage it. These little ones don't know right from wrong. They are in a stage of innocence.

4. The first year is the most critical year of one's whole life. How the infant and young child experience care giving is directly related to how that youngster will perceive God.

5. Be fully involved in your infant's spiritual nurture, for which you are responsible. Be aware that spiritual development is part of a whole and begins at birth.

6. Sometimes, as we reflect on our mistakes, we may wish we could do it over again. But if we had a second chance, we'd make other errors. This recognition keeps us humble. Much of what happens in parenting is grace.

7. We may interchange the words "sharing our faith" and "spiritual nurture," but our awareness is raised to another level when we add the term "our child's spirituality."

What then shall we do?

1. Share your faith by building trust; the child needs to perceive you as trustworthy. To build trust, be dependable, available, and nurturing. Think about what this trust building may mean within your particular context and chosen lifestyle. Who will be your child's primary caregiver?

2. Share your faith by affirming that the bonding is two-sided. The infant communicates with you, and you communicate with your child. Body language, voice, touch, and eye contact are means of communicating. Think about ways you can use these mediums to share the faith.

3. Share your faith readily and naturally. During this spiritual stage of innocence, you are building trust, the foundation for faith. You are also learning the skills of faith shar-

ing. Think about what this means for you.

4. Nurture your own personal faith, for you cannot water the virgin grasses when the well is dry. Give priority to several moments of solitude each day. Get on your knees often and pray for your young one. Commit the beginning and end of each day into God's keeping.

For family

Family time

1. *Trust walk.* Take turns blindfolding a child or parent (or extended family member) while another leads that person. State rules for the activity: (a) Older leaders must give clear instructions to the one blindfolded so no one is hurt. (b) Young leaders must stay within a defined circle with simple impediments. (c) Each leader has two minutes before someone else's turn.

When finished, talk about trust. Ask how it felt for child or adult to be led blindfolded or how it felt to be the leader. Talk about these feelings. Ask: "How does Jesus lead or help us?" Validate their expressions even though they may be different from yours. Share your faith by telling ways you have personally experienced Jesus as leader and guide. Hold hands and take turns saying a short prayer. With young children, speak this prayer and ask them to repeat after you: "Thank-you, Jesus, for taking care of us. Amen."

2. *Trust acrostic.* On a large sheet of paper, print the word TRUST vertically. Ask: "What is God like? Can you think of a word starting with T?" Write the word in horizontally and go on to the next letter. When finished, ask what they think these words mean. Share how you have experienced God in any one of these ways. Hang the acrostic as a "God reminder."

3. *Family grace.* Teach this prayer to your young children and say it before each meal: "God loves me, I love God.

Thank-you, thank-you for this food. Amen." Occasionally, suggest other words for the first line such as "God made me, God gives friends," and ask them to add their own words of thanks before the amen. These may get lengthy but don't curtail them. If you have several children, ask them to take turns on different days.

4. *Memorize a Psalm.* Read Psalm 23:1-3 and memorize this trust psalm. Some ways for fun memorizing are: (a) Print the words on newsprint and read several times. Cover up a noun each time you've read it. After that, cover the verbs. (b) Print the words on newsprint but cut out and glue on pictures for the nouns. Recite several times and then cover up one picture at a time. Recite from memory.

Next, hear their ideas and explain words like shepherd, pasture, waters, restores (refreshes) my soul, and righteousness. Turn the newsprint over, divide into sections, and ask each person to draw a picture about the psalm. Members (including parents) share what they've drawn.

5. *Family chain.* Cut a 4- by 36-inch strip from a roll of brown wrapping paper. Fold this strip back and forth into 3-inch accordion pleats. Cut a human figure pattern, impose on the pleated sheet and cut out, leaving it connected at hands and feet. Pull it apart and you will have a human chain. Note how families are God's special idea and each person in a family is special. Ask each member to choose a figure on the chain and draw/color in features and clothes of him or herself. You will have undrawn figures left. Note that God's family is large and many special people can be added to your family. Ask for suggestions about whom to include. The one suggesting completes that figure. Lay the chain on the table and ask each member to pick one or two persons to pray for (make sure all chain members are included). Take turns saying short prayers for those selected.

Celebrate the family

Celebrate *"Birth or Adoption Day."* Bake a cake and decorate the room with streamers and balloons. Inform everyone that the family is celebrating everybody's birthday or adoption day the way we celebrate Jesus' birthday, that this is a party where family members (or extended family) will talk and share about being adopted or born. Begin by looking at yours and the children's earliest pictures and cards. If you have any artifacts of the children or yourself such as toys, books, dresses, or shoes, show these too.

The parent becomes the main storyteller. Begin with your infancy stories (if possible, invite your parents or siblings over to help tell your stories). Move on to the story of each child. Detail where you were living, where the child was born or adopted, and what was exciting about this new family member. Preschoolers enjoy these moments in the sun. Invite older children to add their memories of a younger sibling's addition to the family. If you have mixed-race or other nationality adoptions, you will want to focus on the specialness of that culture. Let your children know how glad you are that each one is a part of this family. To the tune of "Happy Birthday," make up your own family song.

An idea for a family night activity

Grandparent faith stories. Invite your parents or other older persons to your home and spend an evening together talking and playing games. At least a week in advance, ask the guests to prepare personal stories they would like to tell. Suggest that they share life experiences, including anecdotes about answered prayers and other faith stories.

For study

Search the Scriptures

"On the eighth day, when it was time to circumcise him, he was named Jesus.... When the time of their purification according to the Law of Moses had been completed, Joseph and Mary took him to Jerusalem to present him to the Lord ... and to offer a sacrifice in keeping with what is said in the Law of the Lord" (Luke 2:21-24).

List ways these parents took spiritual responsibility for their infant.

What were these parents communicating to the child Jesus about their strong Jewish faith?

Discuss the questions

1. Discuss: "The way the infant and young child experience the care-giving parent is directly related to how that youngster will perceive God."

2. How do you respond to the statement "Much of what happens in parenting is sheer grace."

Engage in group response

1. What does the word "trust" mean to you? Whom do you trust? What is your earliest recollection of finding someone trustworthy?

2. Identify a family incident that involved trust or lack of it. Find a partner (other than a spouse). Share your stories with each other and act out one incident at a time for the group. In each case, the parent plays the child role and the partner, the parent role. The child convinces the parent that he/she has proven to be trustworthy or untrustworthy. What insights have you gained?

3. Are you trustworthy? With crayons, draw a large heart. Inside the heart, sketch symbols to represent five areas in which you consider yourself trustworthy. Share your symbols with the group.

Chapter 4

Young Saplings

*Emotional, Spiritual, and Moral
Development of Children from Eighteen
Months to Five Years of Age*

At the edge of the woods

Yºou've walked down the lane through the virgin grasses
and are ready to step onto the shaded path winding
between the green, moss-covered trunks of forest
pines. But, stop. Don't go yet. Look what's growing here on
the edge of the woods! Saplings, all sizes and heights. Glis-
tening green leaves whisper in the tender branches. Slender
tree trunks of different sizes and shapes—some straight, some
bent, some hiding in the shade of a weathered oak, some
growing in clusters, others standing apart—take their places
like guards of a future adolescence. It's as though they should
all be wearing a sign that reads "Beware, new life growing
here."

These immature saplings are not unlike your young child eagerly moving through the years toward greater independence, a person with whom you will be sharing your faith now and in the years ahead. At times you may feel overwhelmed. As one young mother said, "My two-year-old is so active, some mornings I don't want to get up!" Inevitably, parents of this age-group ask many questions.

What if my child's development doesn't fit the prescription?

Don't worry about it! You can't make growth happen. He'll get there in his own time. The early months have only introduced you to parenthood. You have been touched by the incredible "firsts" your baby–this God-invention–has gone through during the first eighteen months. What you may not have noticed is that each of these firsts marks the beginning of moving away from dependence.

It's rather breathtaking to think of all the adjustments parents have to make. A child changes and takes longer and faster steps toward an independence which ultimately will be achieved in about nineteen or twenty years. These young ones need, year by year, to move through emotional, spiritual, social, moral, and physical stages of growth. Though following God's general pattern for development, that process for each child will be as uneven and individual as that of the young saplings near the woods.

Remember, God is a creative genius who doesn't believe in cloning. Each child is unique, growing at his or her special pace in each area. One active youngster may walk and run at a young age, whereas another talks early. Some three- or four-year-olds may engage in their own prayers, thanking Jesus for everything from parents to peas, whereas another may prefer a taught prayer.

To answer more of those questions simmering in your mind, let's take a brief look at the emotional, moral, and faith development of your child between eighteen months and five years of age. In doing so, we will also look at ways you can best share your faith with a particular age. From there on, let the wise Holy Spirit guide you.

Do young children have faith?

The understanding of how faith and conscience develop in children is a relatively new concept. It has emerged out of the diversified psychological studies of child development, also a young science on the continuum of history. The studies suggest that all areas of development are interrelated. Faith exists even in young children, but within the capacity of the child's experience based on age or overall stage of development.

Do young children have faith? Yes, but not the faith of an adult. Westerhoff calls the faith of young childhood "experienced faith" (*Will Our Children Have Faith?* Seabury Press, 1976). Kropf calls it "heart faith" (*Upon These Doorposts,* Faith & Life Press, 1980). The very young are in a stage of innocence. Trust and worth are key faith words for those under school age. Within these experienced or heart faith stages, you have the responsibility of building trust and worth in your child as she gradually begins to assimilate your faith life and is able to transfer these feelings into faith in God.

As in all areas of development, the definitions are only an attempt to help discern how faith develops and grows in the child. They are not a box into which you cram your young one but more like a compass to guide your understanding. The intent is to help communicate faith and give religious instruction to children in age-appropriate ways.

It is critical to share your faith on a level your child can grasp. A comparison of the three charts referred to in What

Then Shall We Do? near the end of this chapter (page 00) contains an implicit warning against expecting responses from a child that are beyond him. We may impose faith concepts on a child which he cannot understand (for example, expecting a preschool-aged child to take on a head faith which can only be grasped by a much older child). This may not only lead to a pseudo faith, one in which the child mimics what the adult has told him, but may suppress the joy and innocence of experienced faith which are so basic to the next stages.

Do young children know right from wrong?

Like faith responses, moral behavior is closely related to a child's cognitive capacity based on age and development. Kohlberg's research tells us that from infancy to about four years of age, the child is in a premoral level of development. She is not able to reason about right or wrong because cognitive abilities begin to develop later. For the infant or toddler, bad is unpleasant: a wet diaper, an "ouchie," or parents leaving. Good is pleasant: food, shelter, love, or laughter. Right or wrong are determined by how the environment affects her self-centered world (Kohlberg in *Upon These Doorposts*). That's how God created these young developers; they are following divine orders for growth.

At three and four years of age, the child moves towards the preconventional level. During these months and the years ahead, he will develop and expand moral thinking. Now, the child begins to do right because of the consequences to himself. Doing what pleases the parents brings approval and avoids disapproval. This youngster, however, does not yet act out of respect for rules, but only in terms of what's in it for him.

As you relate to your young children, remember: They are not yet ready to engage in moral reasoning, nor do they understand motive. So their sense of right and wrong may be quite different from yours. For example, young Elisa was asked to get some eggs from the fridge. Upset, she got out the eggs, looked at her mother defiantly, took one, and whammed it onto the floor. Robbie was given the same task, but he accidentally dropped the carton and all the eggs broke. If you were to ask five-year-olds which one did the greater wrong, they probably would say "Robbie, because he broke the most eggs." In their concrete world they saw only the amount of damage, not the reasons for the behavior.

What are the faith steps for eighteen months to five years?

Having discussed faith and conscience in young children, let's focus more directly on the faith *development* of the younger child. As young children grow and develop, they become more independent. It is one of their God-given directives. Now the faith task of parents is to build on earlier trust and affirm the child's worth.

How do you develop a sense of worth? First of all, in your own life and relationships—in your faith journey with Jesus Christ—you need to believe that you are a worthy person. Parents who act out of their own sense of worth communicate this by the way they relate to the child. That, in turn, affects the child's present and future faith experience.

A sense of worth is also gained when the young child achieves the next emotional stages of development, which, according to Erikson, begin with *autonomy* at eighteen months and *initiative* at about four years of age (*Childhood and Society,* W. W. Norton and Co., 1963). This child is developing according to her God-given rhythm. This growth is not a smooth, even path. It is more like a rocky road alternating with occasional shaded lanes. As a parent, you do well to realize that the child's inner clock dictates times of disequilibrium during growth spurts followed by phases of equilibrium and calm, each as predictable as the waxing and waning of the moon. The former usually appears at about the half year— one and a half, two and a half (The Gesell Institute's *Child Behavior*, Harper and Row, 1955).

I cannot stress enough the faith-building tasks of parents for this age-group. Faith building requires involved parents who affirm the child's worth and create a home environment where faith growth and sharing are encouraged and celebrated. Let's look at these possibilities in more detail.

How can I share my faith with twos and threes?

At about eighteen months, the small tornado moves in. There is bang and clatter wherever you go. This child is about the task of gaining *autonomy*. The contented baby, now in a phase of disequilibrium, is trying on the world, using all five senses, with the cooperation of a body that is actively on the go. This is God's learning pattern. Parents' admonitions mean little to this child because she hasn't mastered language skills. I suggest you childproof your home and give her areas where she can explore to her heart's content.

Because the toddler is being confronted by a new world, he has a hard time handling too many changes, and you may find him rebelling against sudden change or hurry. Because of limited language, he may react by screaming, lying down and kicking, running away, or pulling off one sock while you put on the other one. He can't be reached by verbal persuasion. So, say a consistent "no" in a few areas really important to you or where he could be harmed. To define limits, pick him up and move him, or distract him to change behavior.

This is often a difficult time for parents, especially if they don't understand what is happening. But if autonomy is not respected, children who constantly hear "no," are told they are "bad," or are readily punished develop a sense of *shame* and *doubt*. This makes it hard for them to achieve the next stage because they become fearful and unsure of themselves.

At two, there is a pleasant lull as she becomes more attuned to all the newness and gains language skills. But at two and a half comes the next growth spurt characterized by the word *no!* Her life is filled with paradox and extremes, bouncing back and forth like a ping-pong ball. Don't shame your child or call her bad, because what she's doing is normal for growth. Set reasonable limits, primarily those activities which could harm the child, and be consistent in your own nay-saying. Encourage appropriate autonomy using affirmative words, behavior, and body language that builds trust and worth in the child. Model God's unconditional love. Instead of saying, "You are a bad girl" (a moral judgment), kneel, use eye contact, firmly hold her hands and say, "I love you very much, but I will not let you hit Sarah." If that doesn't work, remove her and engage her in another activity. Providing secure limits, while nourishing the child's need for acceptance, is a parental juggling act. But it already provides the basis for later belief in a loving, forgiving God rather than a rejecting, punitive one. It takes much wisdom to guide a child through this stage. Too much freedom can be as frightening for the child as too little.

How then can you help with faith growth? With your pre-two, provide activities: walk with him, hold, play, sing, and laugh with him. As this child nears two, he mimics well and can learn short phrases such as "Jesus loves me" or a simple table grace such as "Thank-you, Jesus, for lunch." Or he may identify pictures as you read to him.

By two, your child becomes more verbal. Now you can talk and be understood as you walk. Point out a flower and say words such as "God made this flower. God loves you." Read books to her like *The World God Made* by Cooner (Word,

1994). By two, she can handle a simple tape recorder. Provide tapes (check with your denominational bookstore or curriculum) or record your own stories and songs (make up simple songs about God and insert the child's name). Recently, I listened to a recording of a two-year-old who recited a table grace and sang several short songs about Jesus.

As a youngster moves towards three, she likes to act out simple stories or games and do easy finger plays. It is important to hold your child and read many stories over and over again. Read materials that emphasize parental and God's love in a variety of ways. Sing favorites with your child. Keep a calming environment during your child's difficult developmental periods. Singing instructions is sometimes more productive than merely saying them.

At three, the process of building worth and allowing appropriate autonomy continues. But now the child has a larger world, better language skills, and greater ability to understand. The three-year-old is quite verbal, eager to learn and please, and obedient, following the moral code of the parents. He loves to act out stories, is more able to share, likes to help the parent, and begins to speak his own prayers/grace (which sometimes get quite long). If you read Bible stories to him, he will have a favorite that he wants to hear over and over again. This age is delightful, but six months later a new insecurity strikes. This new stage often is characterized by crying, indicating that the child needs special care and reassurance. What better reassurance of his specialness as God's creation can you give than your love?

How can I share my faith with fours and fives

The child from about four to six years wants to achieve *initiative;* she needs to begin acting on her own and be affirmed for it. Too often, well-meaning parents squelch the faith development of their child at this point, not only because they need control but also because they are acting out of their own fears about the child's well-being. This control instinct negatively affects the child's sense of worth. Thus a four-year-old who tries to do something on her own and is not trusted to do so may become passive and live with inner *guilt* because she may consider acting on her own as wrong.

A four-year-old is maturing. Change and growth are not as dramatic as earlier. He likes to play with a few friends, shares, and is outgoing. He has a vivid imagination and may often tell "tall tales" or have imaginary playmates. Our friend's daughter had a blue kitten under the piano which I was allowed to pet. Another four-year-old had an invisible friend, George, who was given a chair and a plate at the table. They are not lying! Stern reprimands are not needed. Learning to distinguish between reality and unreality is part of the development process. Draw limits if fantasy gets excessive, or distract the child by going into a discussion about something else. This age likes discussing things.

A four-year-old understands that God created the world, made and takes care of her, and wants us to love God, be kind, and share with others. Provide books, games, tapes, videos, and other resources that enhance her faith world and involve her in various religious rituals you practice in your home. Encourage and affirm initiative in tasks, creativity, and play.

A five-year-old is easy to relate to—a breather for parents. He has a good memory, is affectionate, and wants to please (but tends to blame others when something goes wrong). You can see a slow development of cognitive ability, even though his inquisitive questions and general life view are concrete.

By five, your child may begin to wonder what God looks like. (Will God read your letter?) She thinks and talks about heaven in tangible terms. My niece, age five, said to me, "When people die, God puts them into a big airplane and takes them up, up. Then God pokes a hole in a cloud and puts them into a big, soft nest."

You have wonderful opportunity here to provide stories, tapes, discussions, songs, and other resources as you help your child develop skills in initiative that will increase his sense of self-worth. He enjoys books like *My Secret Place* by Magnus (Lothrop, Lee and Shepard Books, 1994) and others. A five-year-old can lead your family council, suggest ideas for family activities, memorize songs and stories, engage in family rituals such as the lighting of the Advent candles or thanksgiving prayers, or draw a picture about Jesus' birth. His good memory creates a basis on which to build new faith experiences.

Tell and read many stories to her. You may find your five-year-old quite ready to share thoughts and questions about God, Jesus, and prayer. Build her sense of worth by careful listening. Ask questions to accelerate and stimulate her thoughts about God, but never say, "No, that's wrong." Your child's understandings of God are developing based on experiences and observations and will go through many changes during the years to come.

Do young children have spiritual experiences?

Jesus says of the little children, "The kingdom of heaven belongs to such as these" (Matthew 19:14), and the psalmist proclaims, "From the lips of children and infants you [Lord] have ordained praise" (Psalm 8:2). Children are not only moral beings but have within them an innate spiritual center. God is at work even in our youngest ones whether we share our faith with them or not.

Visions of Innocence by Hoffman (Shambhala, 1992) recounts many pages of personal incidents told by adults of all ages who recall early spiritual experiences. Try to think back. Were there such experiences in your early life? Remembering them may sensitize you to your child's spirituality. I recall several, one deeply etched in my mind: When I was three, home was a cottage beside a creek, near a poplar woods. One afternoon, I was sitting on the south side, leaning against the wall, warmed by the bright spring sunshine. Birds (probably swallows) flew back and forth between the woods and the cottage eaves. I didn't know color, but in my mind's eye they were a fluorescent pink and sky blue. The beauty of the birds, the quiet woods, and the warm sky flooded into one whole, and I was captivated and immersed in a feeling of peace, wholeness, and serenity. To this day, I have never been able to recapture that feeling, despite my yearnings. Today I call it a God experience.

A child may not be able to identify or relate an incident as a God encounter, but it is possible that our children may have profound spiritual experiences. We will never know about most of them. Children three or older may engage in reflections about God that we know come from a deeper source. Listen to these children, take their words seriously, and affirm God's love for them. Use moments like this to say together a "God thank-you."

Travel tips

You've stood beside these young saplings for a long time, deeply engrossed in all the changes your young ones are growing through. As you journey on, through the greening woods, let me reinforce again the importance of gaining an understanding of your child's development stages.

- Being aware of the different stages of change and growth gives you a platform from which to operate. It warns against trying to make a pseudo adult of your young one. When we try to force maturation in a child beyond her years, we may be meeting our own needs, not the child's.

- Being aware of the different stages of change and growth alerts you to the fact that all stages are normal processes and cannot be skipped. At the same time, recognizing that these stages are not rigid gives you flexibility to treat each child according to the individual's needs.

- Being aware of the different steps of development helps you realize that no two children are alike. Don't judge your child's development by what others are doing, but rather focus on this particular child.

- Being aware of the different stages of development helps you understand the possible moral and faith capabilities of a child. This awareness helps you identify resources to use and also the type of questions about God to anticipate.

For review and response

Recap

1. Our young ones need to move, year by year, through emotional, spiritual, social, moral, and physical stages of growth. Although following God's general pattern for development, that process for each child will be uneven and individual.

2. Faith exists even in young children but within the capacity of the child's experience based on age or stage of development.

3. The young one is not able to reason about what is right or wrong because cognitive abilities develop later.

4. As you relate to your young children, remember, they are not yet ready to engage in moral reasoning nor do they understand motive, so their sense of right and wrong may be quite different from yours.

5. As children grow, they are bound to try on the world and seek a new independence. Now the faith task of parents

becomes that of building a sense of worth.

6. Parents do well to realize that the child's inner clock dictates times of disequilibrium during growth spurts, followed by phases of equilibrium and calm.

What then shall we do?

1. Take five to ten minutes a day to nurture your own faith and find an inner serenity. Getting your bearings will strengthen your ability to cope. Close your eyes and quietly recite Psalm 23. Find that quiet meadow in your mind. Visualize the scene using all five senses. Picture Jesus present, his hand on your shoulder. Relax. Feel his divine presence empowering you.

2. Review this chapter repeatedly to help you understand the overall development of your child. Focus specifically on the age your child is now. Put into action the suggestions for appropriate sharing of faith, and think of other ways this can be done. Keep the child's faith-building tasks in mind.

3. To learn more about the areas of development, read books by Gesell, Erikson, Kohlberg, Westerhoff, and also Lehn's *Children and Faith* (Faith & Life Press, 1994). Study the charts in the Appendix: (a) Erikson's Developmental Tasks, (b) Westerhoff's and Kropf's Spiritual Dimensions of Faith, and (c) A Comparative Chart of the Developmental Patterns of Growth.

For family

Family time

1. *Hand pictures.* On white paper, draw around the hands of your young child. Cut out and glue onto construction paper. Punch a hole at the top and attach string. On the hand print the name of the child, reciting it aloud to the young one. Below it print "God loves me." Parents make one too. All hold

up their hand picture and say several times, "God loves me."

2. *Act a Bible story.* (This sample is from Exodus 16.) "Mommies, daddies, boys, girls, and babies were walking and walking (hold children's hands and walk). They were carrying heavy bags (give items to each one and groan). Mommies and daddies were moving to a new house. Boys, girls, and babies were tired, hungry, and grumpy (scowl faces). They lay down to sleep (lie on blanket and close eyes. Quietly scatter cereal.) When they awoke, they saw cereal food. Surprise! Let's pick it up. Let's eat our cereal food. (Continue talking while the rest eat.) God sent the cereal food. God took care of the mommies, daddies, boys, girls, and babies. (Optional) God takes care of Mommy, Daddy, _____ and _____ (children's names)."

3. *Seasonal event.* Go for a walk (in autumn rake up leaves and play your own version of Leaf Romp). Ask your children what they see, smell, or hear. Gather leaves, shrubs, or twigs. At home, pile them on the table to make a centerpiece. Talk about how God's world changes with the seasons. In unison, say: "Thank-you, God," and add: "for _____ (the gatherings they brought home)."

4. *Story apron.* Young children love stories, so share your faith through storytelling, biblical or otherwise. Work up a repertoire. Make an apron with a large front pocket. Put artifacts representing each story into the pocket. A child pulls out an item and that story gets told.

5. *Poems and more poems.* Children's books are indicative of young ones' responses to the rhythm and feeling of poetry. Read and recite poetry for fun times, when you're engaged in activites, or riding in the car. As children grow older, recite hymns and introduce your children to good quality poetry such as the Psalms and other classics. Make up poems with your children, including simple poems about

Bible stories or personal faith experiences. Make up rhymes when you give instructions; children are much more likely to respond.

Celebrate the family

Celebrate Epiphany. In some countries, gifts are exchanged on Epiphany, January 6. Epiphany celebrates the visit of the Magi (Matthew 2) and their worship and presentation of gifts to the infant Jesus. Choose one of these to celebrate: (1) Act out the story. Note that gifts for Jesus are not only material things but also our abilities and talents. Draw names and make Promise Booklets containing coupons promising to gift the other in some way through the use of time or abilities. (2) Invite friends for a party and ask them to bring gifts for needy families. Make a huge gold crown and glue a band around it with the words from Matthew 2:11 printed on it. Ask guests to put their gifts into the crown. Serve crown-shaped sugar cookies.

An idea for a family night activity

Single night. Invite a single adult to join you for a picnic. Play suitable outdoor games. (For the preschool age, it could be as simple as forming a circle, sitting in the grass, and rolling a ball to each other.) If this guest seems to enjoy your family, invite him or her to be an extended family member who participates in and contributes to your family activities on a regular basis.

For study

Search the Scriptures

"He [Jesus] took the children in his arms, put his hands

on them and blessed them" (Mark 10:16).

What does Jesus' action say about the role of children in God's kingdom?

What does this story tell you about young children and faith?

Discuss the questions

1. How is the faith of young children different from that of adults?

2. How do the comments on the moral development of young children help you define age-appropriate expectations of your child?

Engage in group response

1. *What do you think?* Young children can be talked into anything by an admired adult. A teacher in the church made her five-year-olds class her mission field. All but one promptly repeated the formulas for conversion. These "saved" children then ostracized the one and told him he was a sinner and would go to hell. Do we engage in emotional abuse when we manipulate youngsters, demanding cognitive faith commitments which even many older children can't comprehend? Discuss.

2. How was worth affirmed in your home? Did your parents encourage autonomy and initiative? If so, how did this affect your faith life? Share with the group. Now think about your children. What would you want to do differently? The same? Write "Parent Commitment" at the top of a sheet of paper, and list five ways in which you want to encourage faith development in your child.

Chapter 5

A Wild Strawberry Patch

*Emotional, Spiritual, and Moral
Development of Children from Five and a
Half to Twelve Years of Age*

....

The sun-drenched clearing

O n the Canadian prairie where I grew up, early summer
often yielded surprises in the low-lying hay sloughs.
Under the shaved grasses drying in the sun, we discovered countless patches of wild strawberries–red berries
dripping with color, closely grouped with smaller berries not
quite ripe or white blossoms awaiting their debut. How well I
remember the sight and taste of those succulent berries. Now,
in this very moment, as you walk down the path, the young
saplings behind you, memory stirs again. You and your children have reached a sun-drenched, grassy clearing in the

woods, and there they are! Patches of strawberries wherever you look! They cling together in their little circles. Blossoms lift chubby faces to the sun and revel in their wide world of longer days and shorter nights. In the quiet of a summer morning, you hear the invitation to stop. Please do. Make your baby comfortable on a blanket and encourage your children to enjoy this gift of nature. This is only one of God's miracles.

Our children are also God's miracles. In many ways, children ages five and a half to twelve are not too different from these wild strawberry patches. Children after age five exude life and energy not unlike these closely knit berries in different stages of maturation. In the midst of their liveliness, eagerness, and expanding friendships, the agenda for you and these older children is beginning to change as they become increasingly independent. Through school, church, and play, as well as the influence of media and community, they are exposed to many more values and ideas than your own.

At times, we may become somewhat anxious during these years. We are losing control. We may not like some of the outside influences affecting our children. We wish we could protect and immunize them from the pains and tragedies of our modern society. We can't do that, but we *can* provide a loving Christian home, which like a bastion or fortress provides a sanctuary where our child finds trust, worth, and security—a dependable place where faith is found and nurtured, and where no issue or question is off limits.

Today's children face an incredibly complex world. At times you may feel they have more cloud covers than sunny days in their strawberry patch lives. They face questions, distorted values, anxieties, and fears. At times, our answers may not fit, and we will have to struggle along with our children. Yet, even in today's modern, highly technological world with all its social and political problems, God's established patterns for growth and development continue to be basic. The pseudo sophistication, early physical maturity, and broad educational experiences, especially of the preadolescent, may sometimes fool us into believing children are more mature than they really are.

Yet, according to emotional, moral, and faith development theories, each child must process those stages and needs to have time to do so. That's how God made them. It could well be that through crisis, media influence, peer pressure, and "street smarts," some of our children are growing up much too fast, at least outwardly. That's why parents need to continue being aware of their children's spiritual, moral, and emotional needs so that you can relate to these young ones' lives and nurture their spiritual growth *where they are.*

It is a challenge for parents to grow in their faith and think through how that faith relates to the environment in which they and their children live and move. The simplistic, naive ideas some of us remember from children's Sunday school may not be adequate for the child in today's world. It's time for us to redefine the meaning of our faith for the twenty-first century. It is out of this context that your questions may be emerging, some of them asking for reassurance, others for information or understanding.

What are the moral stages of this older age-group?

Children between ages five and a half and twelve are in process, never the same person today as they were yesterday. If this growth were steady, we would be better equipped to know what to expect. But growth is uneven, and, though not as pronounced as earlier, times of disequilibrium continue to announce that a fresh spurt, a new change, is taking place. Older children are steadily moving toward the teen years, when major transitions will propel them towards young adulthood.

The thought of pending disequilibrium may be rather disconcerting for parents, because we just discussed the gentle, pleasing fives in the last chapter. We want to say, "May I breathe now?" as though we've reached our mountaintop. The most demanding physical caregiver days may be over, but the years ahead continue to require a full commitment. It's not a time of less parenting; it's simply different. Just when we think we've mastered the skills, we are again challenged to change gears and grow with the child. Each stage of their childhood requires changes in the way we relate, view moral expectations, or share the faith.

After age five, the moral reasoning of a child continues at the *preconventional* level (described in the previous chapter). But new understandings emerge as your child's ability to reason, think, and make choices grows. At this age, she is still quite focused on self and does the "right" thing to avoid the consequences. Good behavior may be a way of getting what she wants. During early school years, the idea of something being wrong if you get caught surfaces frequently. If Jeff has his hands in the cookie jar and gets away with it, it's okay. But if he gets caught, it's wrong.

During preadolescent years, the young person, more aware of the larger world, begins to understand the need for rules and will respect them. The teaching of parents or the church and the laws of society are to be obeyed because that's the right thing to do. At this *conventional* level, motives for good behavior or conformity are based on getting approval.

What are the faith stages of this older age-group

As your child matures in her understandings of right and wrong, she also grows into the next *faith stage*. According to Westerhoff, children remain at the *experience* level or *heart faith* (Kropf) during the earlier years. But, remember, this is a process, not an event. As you continue to affirm your child's worth and encourage her to achieve initiative, you will notice a shift toward more mature behavior. This doesn't mean she's grown up. It only means she's moving in the right direction according to God's good ideas for emotional growth and spiritual development.

During the years that follow, you will notice changes in your child. Although he is continuing to *experience* faith, the larger world he now enters propels him towards the next faith stage, that of *belonging*. According to Erikson, he is also becoming increasingly *industrious*. If the earlier faith stages and the accompanying emotional tasks have been well built, your child will now have a feeling of well-being as he develops a sense of belonging to God, the family, church, and friends. It is important for your family to be part of a warm church community where this sense of belonging can develop and grow.

As you spiritually nurture your child, you need to affirm her sense of belonging and show appreciation for the industrious behavior of this energetic, enthusiastic age. For example, eight-year-old Maria baked her first cake, and her father praised her. Her eyes sparkled. Now she was ready to try other new things. However, if earlier stages of trust, autonomy, and initiative have not been accomplished, the child may feel inferior and have inner doubts about her ability to accomplish a task.

During preadolescence, beginning at about age eleven, other changes take place. Although faith is still primarily experienced and a sense of belonging is important, your older child is growing toward the teens and an *affiliative* (Westerhoff) or *head* faith (Kropf). Now *identity* issues surface (Erikson), and faith tasks are best characterized by the word *inquiry*. As in the previous example, if earlier stages haven't been achieved, the preteen experiences not only inferiority but also moves towards identity confusion and its related problems.

During preadolescence, children may affiliate with the church and its teachings, are clearer about right and wrong, and may logically think through faith issues. These children moving toward the teens ask many questions about God. (Luke 2:46 demonstrates the faith concerns of a bright, spiritually nurtured and stimulated twelve-year-old.) Questions about drugs, relationships, sex, HIV, etc., and how they relate to faith may emerge early in today's preadolescents because of their accelerated physical, social, and intellectual development and the influences of media. Be a good listener. Encourage questions. Ask thought-provoking questions, but don't be overeager, overtalkative, or overmoralizing. When a child feels pushed, he or she will turn you off.

Many preadolescents will continue to build on the experienced faith of earlier childhood and grow toward a maturing faith without what some call a conversion experience. Others may begin to think of wrong not only as an individual act but also as an inner force that misleads them (the Greek word for sin means "to miss the mark"). These older children or early teens may feel urged to commit their lives to Jesus Christ. The significance of this commitment matures with years, but the decision is a beginning that gives a focus and direction to life. As I stated in chapter 1, there is no *one way* to experience faith, because God touches lives at different times, in different ways. Be aware that the beliefs of your denomination or those emphasized in your home will also affect how your growing child perceives the nature of a spiritual decision at this age.

How can I share faith with five-and-a-half-year-olds through seven-year-olds?

When we talk about sharing our faith with a particular age-group, it is helpful to know some of the characteristics of these berries growing in their strawberry patch, all at different stages of development. The berry patch imagery helps remind us that we're talking about growth and change, not wax museum replicas. All children will develop at their own rate, and the guidelines are there to help raise our awareness. Reflect on the following:

If you thought Easy Street was here at age five, you can put your hiking boots back on because at age five and a half to six, change strikes again, characterized by the extremes of the two-year-old, with the addition of combative language. He reacts to criticism, feels easily overwhelmed, and may dawdle as a means of coping. I suggest you pick your battles and impose natural consequences (see chapter 10) when boundaries are stretched too far, because spanking (if you're a spanker) does no good. Remember, this child is not being bad but is dealing the best he can with the next growing pains God visits on this age.

Your child at this age understands that God is creator, loves her, her family and friends, and she knows how to be kind and sharing. Prayer for herself and others is important. She likes Bible stories (has favorite ones) and because of polarized thinking is vulnerable to teachings about the devil. My response would be, "The Bible doesn't say much about the devil, but it says a lot about the God who is much stronger, who made the whole world, and loves and takes care of us." Help her with faith questions. Encourage trust in Jesus and daily prayer.

Loosen your laces because at age seven, your child relates warmly, listens well (although more self-absorbed and forgetful). He may worry at times, especially about trying new things. But on the whole, his quieter, more thoughtful ways make him easy to have around. Books like *I'd Choose You: Giving the Blessing to Your Child* by Trent (Word, 1994) help affirm his worth. Now your child may begin to have some ideas about what bad and good means. He rarely needs to be disciplined, is becoming conscientious about stealing, cheating, or lying, and has many questions about God. He may lose his innocent faith in God and the "realness" experienced earlier and may even stop praying. Express your loving care and share God's loving care with him. Share experiences about how God answers your prayers. Try to rekindle the God-child relationship by holding his hands after a good day and together thanking God.

How can I share faith with eight-to ten-year-olds?

Your child is now working at faith tasks of *belonging* and emotional issues of *industry*, bringing you into a new, exciting phase of faith sharing. At age eight, the quiet one becomes energetic and robust, doesn't want to be told what to do, and is demanding of the caregiver's attention. Your child at this age thrives on praise and can be guided by being deprived of a favorite item or activity. She's very interested in religion (particularly heaven) and likes to learn from the Bible and memorize. She may feel shame when she's done wrong but isn't sure how to make things better.

At age nine, your child is strongly self-motivated, ambitious, and honest. Your nine-year-old begins to detect shades of right and wrong and wants to be trusted. If he does wrong, his conscience may sometimes lead him to tell a parent. Strangely enough, this self-reliant young one may suddenly lose interest in God and only pray when a need is sensed.

At age ten, you have a social, amiable young person in your home who likes to memorize and learn facts. She takes a firm stand on what she believes is wrong or right, but acceptance by friends comes first. So she may call in adult authority with statements such as "My Dad says ..." etc., to take the pressure off herself. The ten-year-old lives in the "now" and, consequently, doesn't think much about God, death, or other deeper subjects. She may think of God as a spirit (which may contribute to the impersonal feeling towards God) yet still believes that if her prayer is answered, God did it.

Your child between ages eight and ten provides fertile years for sharing your faith. These are great times for discussion, sharing your own faith story and experiences, reading, learning the stories of others, and joining in family service projects. Modeling the Christian life is as important as talking about it. If he has friends in the church, he will be eager to be part of the church, attend camp, or any other activities provided. Open your home to his friends and include those friends in family rituals, where suitable.

How can I share faith with eleven- to twelve-year-olds?

You will see some decided changes as your child, with whom you can now reason well, moves toward and into a *head* or *affiliative* stage of faith. Changes will vary from child to child and month to month. Some girls reach puberty early and others do not. Boys tend to develop more slowly.

Relate to your preadolescent as an individual, and do much sensitive listening to help you understand the particular questions or issues she is dealing with. Take advantage of these years because at this age, they may still come to you with their questions and concerns. When the teen years arrive, they begin to withdraw from you and turn to their peers.

The eleven-year-old is talkative, social, and, at times, moody. It is a change time, and he needs much parental support. Combative behavior may merely be an expression of inner confusion as he begins his search for self. This age wants to be treated fairly and talked with, not to. He may see God as a spirit who doesn't influence his life and prays when he wants something. He may like brief pertinent worship experiences (remember this for family devotions) and church-related events, if they include his friends. This age may have already experienced some of life's pain. He needs your reassurance and a witness to the fact that God is constantly loving and working for good. Help him understand that God does not send evil but allows evil to happen because humans have been given the freedom to choose, and they often make bad, even wicked, choices. Explain to him that natural disasters such as tornadoes, earthquakes, and blizzards are not visited on people by God. They are natural processes of nature that *become* disasters for people who live in those places. Take full advantage of opportunities for discussion.

At age twelve, your child is more mature, more cooperative, and less self-centered. Peer approval is important and relationships more developed. The tasks—faith, moral, and emotional—are similar to age eleven, yet more expansive. Her conscience is more developed, and she begins to conceptualize and wonder more about what it's like to die, about God, and other religious issues. Many will readily accept the religious teachings of the church and home, and some will start doing some serious thinking about religious concerns and questions. She may believe that thinking about God makes you feel good, that prayer helps you, and that God is an important part of one's life.

Encourage growth through participation in church-related groups. Provide good reading materials, and be available to talk things through. By prayer and sensitivity to the Spirit, be aware of and take time for your child's questions. Sometimes these questions may be subtle, and you need to lis-

ten for the feelings behind the words. You will help his faith
grow by not merely giving answers but by responding with
open-ended questions that prompt him to think.

There may come a time, when she has initiated a discussion, that you feel prompted to ask: "Why, do you think, do
people decide to be Christians?" Don't push; let her talk. Be
inwardly at prayer, as your child makes decisions to move forward in her faith.

How do spiritual experiences strengthen a child's faith?

Each child, regardless of age, should carry a placard that
reads: HANDLE WITH CARE. GOD AT WORK. It is both hum-
bling and exhilarating to acknowledge that our children may
experience God in surprising ways far beyond limitations of
faith development stages or parental expectations. A child's
capacity for wonder, curiosity, the sense of miracle, mystery,
fantasy, and awe—so much a part of childhood—makes her or
him capable of absorbing myth as subjective reality in a way our
logical adult minds have long forgotten how to fathom. Don't
you sometimes yearn for a sense of the magic and mystery of
childhood, which years ago became blurred by so-called reality?

We can't go back, but we can be rejuvenated by our
children's spiritual experiences, which strengthen their faith
and ours. Years ago, our kindergartner came home and in an
awed voice said, "Tommy showed me his marble today; it has
a hole in it. If you put it real close to your eye, you can see Jesus
having his last lunch with his friends." I was deeply touched.
Jesus hinted at a childlike spirituality available for those who
trust implicitly and observe through eyes of wonder.

Sometimes our children are catapulted into a new spiritual experience through crisis. Margaret tells this story: "I was
seven and drove to school in a horse-drawn buggy with older

neighbor children. One afternoon, homeward bound, a black cloud loomed over us, and moments later rain and hail pelted down. The horse stopped. 'We've got to pray,' shouted the driver. I said prayers every night but had never *prayed*. Now I prayed! Just like that, the storm stopped and the sun peeked out. I was sure God did it. When I told my parents, they were glad and believed with me. After that, I prayed about anything because I knew God could do it. Later, I was sometimes disappointed," she added, and then, with a twinkle in her eye, said, "But you know, I'm sixty now and when I can't find something, I pray and usually find it. That storm changed my life!"

Children have repeatedly told stories of God experiences, callings, and insights that defy our sense of reality until we realize that faith sharing is not our task alone. Let's never forget the child Jesus' questions in the temple (Luke 2) or the call of young Samuel (1 Samuel 3). May we be awed by the realization that within our growing child moves an innate spirituality where God works out marvels beyond our comprehension.

Travel tips

The virgin grasses, the saplings, and these strawberry patches have given you much to think about as communicators of faith to your children. As you continue your walk through the woods and observe mosses, lichens, and green growing things on the forest floor, reflect on these tips to help you share your faith with your children.

1. Nourish your child's self-esteem. Criticism, put-downs, and making fun of your child undermine confidence. A child has no way of protecting herself against adults. Respect your child's feelings and rights.

2. Empathize with your child. It's not easy being a kid, no matter how much we fantasize about how wonderful our

childhood was. Encourage her to talk out her feelings. Pose open-ended questions that encourage her ideas.

3. Be honest with your own feelings. When we're angry, we readily send blaming *you* messages, like "*You* make me angry." Instead, talk about your feelings, like "*I* feel angry when you walk on the floor with muddy boots."

4. Be aware that your child is learning morality and faith from you. When situations are emotionally laden, he learns and is influenced by how you handle difficult situations. He also observes your failures and dilemmas, and if you share how you felt later or (if it involves your child) even apologize, you are modeling a way of living your faith.

For review and response

Recap

1. Children after age five exude life and energy not unlike these closely knit berries in different stages of maturation. In the midst of their liveliness, eagerness, and expanding friendships, the agenda for you and these older children is beginning to change as they become increasingly independent.

2. The pseudo sophistication, early physical maturity, and broad educational experiences, especially of the preadolescent, may sometimes fool us into believing they're more mature than they really are.

3. The simplistic, naive ideas some of us remember from children's Sunday school may not be adequate for the child in today's world.

4. The most demanding physical caregiver years may be over, but the years ahead continue to require a full commitment. It's not a time of less parenting; it's different.

5. May we be awed by the realization that within our growing child moves an innate spirituality where God works out marvels beyond our comprehension.

What then shall we do?

1. On cards, write Bible verses that affirm worth and belonging. Place in a box on the table. Each morning, all take a verse to read before leaving. Suggest that these are reminders that God is with each one during the day. Reflect on your verse while driving to work or engaging in other tasks.

2. This older group is ready for family devotions (daily or at times designated by you and your family). They should be brief (less than four to five minutes). Focus on worship and select one main thought. For example: Select one verse and ask: "What does this say about God? Has anyone thought of or felt God in this way today (this week)? How? Where? When?" Share briefly, then express a word of thanks. Plug into the ability of older children and suggest that they take turns finding a verse and leading the devotional time.

For family

Family time

1. *God collage.* Ask: "What is God like?" Provide magazines. You and your children each find a picture that may be a symbol of God. For example, "God is like a mother bird. God takes care of us." Paste onto newsprint and share your thoughts with each other. Don't critique your children's views. Your child's perception of God reflects many influences from media, hymns, etc., and will continue to change and mature. Listen, ask questions, and affirm.

2. *Creation awareness.* Experience God's creative force in the world of nature. Deuteronomy 6:5-9 indicates that we're to share the faith while walking on the way (out-of-doors). Children have an awareness of God's presence when they are in the free outdoors and thus praise God (Psalm 8:2). Stimulate observation with questions such as "Who can find something blue?" etc. Go bird-watching with your older children. Make them aware of God's creative genius: God doesn't make clones, and we're even more unique.

3. *Bodybuilding.* Older children want to do good but need guidance. Read Colossians 3:12-15 and excerpts from Matthew 5–7. Note that we do good because we love Jesus and want to act like God's children. Being Christian takes practice just the way bodybuilders or aerobic dancers practice to train their bodies. On paper, each family member draws himself or herself as a bodybuilder or exerciser, and labels each body part with words that depict Christian character, beginning with biblical references and adding their own, such as "respect," "volunteer," "keep promises," etc." Discuss how these could be put into action. Each one makes a weekly promise to exercise one body part. For example, "This week I will turn off the TV and _____ five times." All report back next week and take on a new body-part exercise.

4. *Advent calendar.* Church holidays provide opportunities to share your faith. In the Appendix, you will find Advent calendars with four weeks of activities listed. Choose those that fit your family. Enjoy the season.

5. *Pretzels for Lent.* The faith of older children grows through participation in religious rituals. Make favors for Thanksgiving, write a prayer for Advent devotions, or read Luke 2:1-20 before Christmas gifts are opened.

Consider this Lenten activity: Pretzels are often associated with Lent (perhaps because of simple ingredients sym-

Pretzels

1 tablespoon/5 ml. fast-rising yeast
3/4 cup/175 ml. water
1 tablespoon/5 ml. sugar
1 tablespoon/5 ml. oil
1/4 teaspoon/1 ml. salt
2 cups/500 ml. flour

Mix and knead until smooth, then cut into small pieces. Shape and place on greased cookie sheet. Brush with beaten egg white, sprinkle with coarse salt, and bake at 425F/220C until golden brown.

bolizing fasting and penitence). Help your older children make pretzels.

Celebrate the family

Celebrate the season of Lent. Since the fourth century A.D., churches preparing for the suffering of Jesus' last days have observed a forty-day period before Good Friday called Lent. We can reflect and celebrate because we live on this side of Easter. Lent is a time for prayer, thinking about God, being sorry, asking forgiveness for wrong things we've done, and doing good things for others.

1. Think about Jesus' last days. Once a week have special devotions. Use the following Scriptures and suggested symbols. Talk together about what these symbols mean. Matthew 21:6-9: palm leaves (wave them). Matthew 26:14-16: foil-covered chocolate coins (eat them). John 13:3-5: towel and basin (wash each other's hands). Luke 22:17-19: grape juice and bread (drink and eat together.) Mark:15:20: cross (make small crosses from twigs or popsicle sticks).

2. Think of good things you can do for needy families or for members of your family.

An idea for a family night activity

Reading night. Provide your children with good reading materials. Take your children with you when you visit the Christian bookstore in your area and permit them to buy a book of their choice. Or visit a library and check out books together. Make popcorn and spend a quiet evening reading at home. Agree on a time period. When finished, talk about what you read.

For study

Search the Scriptures

"And the child [Jesus] grew and became strong; he was filled with wisdom, and the grace of God was upon him" (Luke 2:40).

This verse indicates that Jesus grew physically, emotionally, and spiritually. What could have been some factors in his home that might have contributed to this growth?

If the word "grace" is rooted in the concept of a free gift, what does Luke's statement say about the faith experience of the young Jesus? How was God "gracing" this twelve-year-old?

Discuss the questions

1. List the stages of faith development, what ages they pertain to, and how each age experiences God. What have you learned?

2. How do you think a sense of inferiority negatively affects the faith development of children, youth, and adults?

Engage in group response

1. Do our answers fit? Based on Jesus' life and teachings, we have believed that:

- You turn the other cheek. Blessed are the peacemakers. How are our children to deal with the increased violence in schools?
- Be hospitable. How do we ensure our child's safety during our absence? Should they answer the door? the telephone?
- Be kind. How do you tell your child not to trust a neighbor or relative who has a history of sexual abuse and violence?

Share your thoughts with the group. Explore other concerns.

2. Share meaningful faith experiences you've had with your child from ages five and a half to twelve. In a circle of prayer, thank God for your children.

Chapter 6

Diverging Paths

Choices and Decisions in the Faith Life
of Children

....

Which way now?

You and your children have walked for some time,
enjoying the wildflowers along the wayside, the balmy
air, and the warm morning sun. Now you reach a fork
in the path. No signs are visible, and you wonder which route
will lead you through the woods to the meadow beyond. One
path looks well cared for: it has wood chips strewn along the
middle for dry walking on wet days. But it climbs a steep hill
and appears to be turning north. You want to go east. The
other way is narrower, winding into dark, cool underbrush.
You can hear the gurgling river not too far away. The children
beg to splash in the water. But will the downward path, twist-
ing into the dim woods, prove too frightening?

I don't want to add to your confusion, but look around.
There are more than two paths. Behind you is a one-person
trail, probably leading to someone's cabin. The thought of a

friendly host offering cold lemonade to your thirsty group tempts you, but what if you can't find your way back?

Here's another path, wide and grassy, branches bending low on either side, but it looks as if it hasn't been used for a while. Spiderwebs lace across the openings, swinging from flowering bush to bush as bees hum in the blossoms. Does this one lead to a raspberry grove? Think of the fun you and your children could have, picking and eating the rich, red berries. Or do unused trails make you anxious?

To your left, almost lost to view, is another trail. It is narrow, well worn, speckled with animal tracks. Perhaps you could slip up on a doe with her little fawn. Wouldn't the children be delighted? Which way will you go?

As you think about your choices and how your decision will affect the journey, reflect on the many paths that crisscross your life and the lives of your children.

In his poem "The Road Not Taken," Robert Frost wrote about coming upon two roads diverging in the woods and the difference it makes to take the one less traveled. The thought of an unknown route appeals to our adventurous spirit, but it's usually easier to take the well-worn way and not stretch our wings too far. But how do we choose when there are so many paths?

Our children are also faced by many choices that enter their lives, like a network of trails in the woods. Society is becoming increasingly complex. Our children are growing up in a nuclear century, a space age, a technological era, moving onto an information highway that will radically alter the way people relate and think. We may feel left behind with all their talk of computers, bytes, and chips. At the same time, our children are also confronted by many social problems and issues. Some of these touch their lives directly in daily situations, and others, more indirectly through media influence.

Just as you, pausing at this intersection in the woods, are faced by more than two roads, today's children are faced with innumerable paths: personal choices, moral choices, and faith choices that will make a difference in who they are and who they become. Momentarily, you are wowed by the many paths here in the woods. But this confusion is not unlike the daily lives of your children, especially those who have reached school age. Every day they face inner and outer conflicts, wants, desires, and temptations, sometimes with few tools available for resolving them. The rights and wrongs that were once quite clear to us have become rather murky, and even parents get fuzzy about how to resolve some of the issues. Just giving answers, especially after the early years, is no longer sufficient. Our answers may not fit when a child is questioned by others and is taunted and tempted when she has no response beyond "because Mom or Dad said so!" How then, can we help our children learn to make decisions that reflect the Jesus way of life? How can we empower them? What tools can we provide? Are these the questions you ask?

How does self-esteem contribute to a child's ability to make decisions?

We empower our children by building their self-esteem. We also share our faith—faith in God and in our young one that says "You are valued!" Confident children who feel good about themselves will be able to make better decisions than those who experience life otherwise.

The forming of positive self-esteem is an important part of the faith-building stages of our children. It is a biblically based concept. Jesus' teachings put consistent emphasis on the worth and value of the individual, including children. Nurture your child. Create a stimulating environment. Practice acceptance. Live and share your faith. Then she will grow through these stages in a positive manner. You will empower her to become truly human, to experience life abundantly as Jesus promised.

Virginia Satir, in *Peoplemaking* (Science and Behavior Books, 1972) identifies people with high self-esteem as "high pot" people. "Integrity, honesty, responsibility, compassion, and love all flow easily from the person whose pot is high. He feels that he matters, that the world is a better place because he is here.... Appreciating his own worth, he is ready to see and respect the worth of others. He radiates trust and hope" (p. 22).

If the tasks are not accomplished, as is the case with many abused or unnurtured children, self-esteem is low. These "low pot" children haven't learned how to handle life situations. They become survivors guided by fear and insecurity that invariably lead to self-defeating behavior. Satir says, "Because they feel they have little worth, they expect to be cheated, stepped on, deprecated by others. Expecting the worst, they invite it and usually get it. To defend themselves, they hide behind a wall of distrust and sink into the terrible human state of loneliness and isolation" (*ibid.*).

We share our faith when we affirm our child's worth. Yet it is so easy to crush her spontaneity, joy, or esteem when we are angry, impatient, and tired. A middle-aged chaplain said to me, "When I was about eight years old, my father was repairing the car and asked me to hand him a wrench. I gave him the wrong one. His response was, 'Can't you do anything right?'" After a quiet moment, he added, "Those words have haunted me all my life!"

None of us can build complete self-esteem in our child. Even if we do everything right, we can't control our child's responses to us or the larger environment. Bad days and "low pot" times are normal, especially during growing years, change, or crisis. But when "low pot" becomes a life-view, that self-perception crowds out the good feelings and potential with which our Creator has endowed our children. So don't give up on your positive task!

What do values have to do with good choices?

Positive self-esteem is an important factor in the decisions our children make, but it's not enough. Children can't learn to make good decisions without tools and guidance. In a simpler era, in a much smaller world, parents could determine what was right or wrong and the children obeyed those moral codes, often without questioning. Today's parents may have many concerns about what is right or wrong. Even if they have strong beliefs or values, they sometimes are not sure how to communicate them. They resort to moralizing, preaching, shaming, or blaming, with limited results. None of these methods provides our children with age-appropriate tools for making good choices.

Children who've been well taught may know what's expected at home. But when they're with friends, they may not have the wherewithal to make good decisions in situations that don't fit the answers they've been given. As your child grows, she develops an increasing capacity to think things through. In today's complex world, it is critical that you help your child develop a value system commensurate with the level of her cognitive development. Positive values are the basis for good decisions.

Why is it important to identify my values?

Values reinforced by self-esteem undergird good decisions. Parents need to help their children develop values guided by the basic principles taught and lived by Jesus Christ. But how do we do that?

Begin with yourself. We need to define and redefine our own values. It is easy to assume that the values we were taught at home suffice for our children. These values may even be brought into question when you and your spouse clash over inherited values that are not congruent.

Parents from rural communities now living in urban centers are often conflicted about their values, because some of them may not fit or they don't know how to make them fit. Some parents have few tools to assess their belief system, and they become confused in their attempt to become urbanized. They may merely respond to their environment and integrate the values of their surroundings, yet insist that their children maintain the values with which the parents grew up. That doesn't work. Rather than reacting to the environment, it is important for us to take time to think about the essential ingredients of our faith and the values that support our faith life. We need to think seriously about what values we are communicating to our children.

Where do we begin? Find a resource. Study the teaching and life of Jesus. Concentrate on the Great Commandment (Matthew 22:37-39), the Sermon on the Mount (Matthew 5–7), and read the Jesus narratives. In these writings you find the basic principles on which to base decisions. The following are some key words: love, kindness, justice, peace, mercy, compassion, and acceptance. You will also notice that Jesus put these values to work by putting God first, people before laws, and by practicing acceptance of individuals, regardless of age, gender, race, nationality, marital status, social role, or type of employment.

How can we teach values to our children?

By assessing your own values, you are empowered to communicate these beliefs to your child in a consistent manner. Verbally communicating your beliefs is not enough. We must help our child interpret these values in the context of a given situation. He needs to learn how to choose between better and best as well as between right and wrong. This takes time. During your child's early years, values are communicated through the parents, but these are not his values; his develop later.

Ability to make decisions is very limited, even after age three. But when cognitive skills begin to develop, she can slowly learn to own her values. This learning will be spotty. Children still have to go through moral developmental stages. Your child will continue to act in age-appropriate ways; she may alibi, blame, obey rules without questioning why, and often still consider something wrong only if caught. But through family discussions, activities, and learning experiences related to values, this process of value owning can be accelerated. Helping your children develop positive values is a part of sharing your faith.

Here are some ways to communicate values:

Communicate values through modeling. Children respond better to what they observe in another's behavior than what is said. Values are both caught from and taught by parents, but the catching must be consistent with the teaching. We can't teach our children one way but live another.

Communicate values through activities. Make posters or banners during family time that emphasize a family value. For example, I LOVE MY FRIENDS, PEACE IS THE WAY, THE POOR ARE MY BROTHERS AND SISTERS, etc. (Younger children could substitute pictures for some of the words.)

Communicate values through discussion of the media. Watch TV with your children and discuss positive values being shown. Older children can peruse newspapers and clip articles that exhibit strong values. As your family identifies these values, talk about how they relate to your particular beliefs. Also raise your children's awareness of poor or inadequate values (particularly evident in the media), such as half-truths in politics and advertising, consumerism, self-centeredness, disregard of human worth, and abuse of the environment.

Communicate values by providing good books for your children. The courage of Joan of Arc, the commitment of John and Charles Wesley, the concerns of John Knox, and the steadfastness of early Anabaptists are expressions of how persons of faith dealt with difficult situations. Lehn's *Peace Be With You* (Faith & Life Press, 1980) and *I Heard Good News Today* (Faith & Life Press, 1983) as well as Battle's *Armed With Love* (Parthenon, 1973) are excellent resources for older children. Younger children learn from the simple tales of how bunnies, beetles, and bears dealt with situations. The Bible story book *God Keeps His Promise* (Faith & Life Press and Herald Press, 1970) by Lehn is another resource for children ages four to six.

Communicate and establish values through the discussion of dilemmas. The most adequate way for school-aged children to learn to own their values is through the discussion of dilemmas, either personal situations they are facing or something you bring up for discussion during your family time.

When your child or family brings up a personal dilemma, instead of giving answers, process by the use of these questions: "What can you do? What else could you do? What would happen if you do this? What's the best thing about doing it this way? Do you think it would be better to do _____ or _____?" Reflect on the dilemma in the light of value questions, such as "What does this have to do with peace?" "What are ways you can show Robbie you care about him, even after you ask him to return the toy he stole from you?" Reflect with your child on values involved. Pray with your child about a dilemma she is trying to resolve. Dealing with dilemmas helps build a value system that is closely connected to real-life decision making.

Another way to teach values is to consider the dilemma of others. For example: Charlie, age nine, wanted to be a member of a club. Club members invited him. "May my best friend, Rudy, come?" he asked. The boys say, "No. Rudy is black." What should Charlie do?

To further establish values, discuss questions, such as "What is better, to do your homework or visit a sick friend?" Many other exercises, dilemmas, and questions are available in Simon's *Helping Your Child Find Values to Live By* (Simon & Schuster, 1991).

What do we mean by age-appropriate decisions?

When we talk about self-esteem and the building of a value system as a basis for making decisions, we need to remember that we're talking about a process, not an event. In the early years, self-esteem and values are communicated from the parent to the child through the bonding relationship. Young children don't make decisions; they respond to their environment. Parents need to understand the capacity of the child. Don't overwhelm an eighteen-month-old with choices for which she's not ready. I followed a young father through the supermarket recently as he asked his toddler in the cart, "Which cookies do you want?" "Which cereal shall we buy?" The baffled child didn't respond.

By age three (or late two), a child may be ready to choose between two items. "Do you want this shirt or that one?" I watched a mother open the closet door and ask, "Which dress do you want to wear?" The child took her mother through the paces as she decided and repeatedly changed her mind.

As you become aware of your child's cognitive ability, you will also be able to help him develop tools for decision making by asking these questions: "What can you do? What would happen if? What will you do?" During early school years, you can make a game of it while walking or traveling by asking "What would happen if?" By doing this, you stretch your child's thinking.

As our children grow older, we can use the dilemma approach, but we can also introduce a more sophisticated tool. Give her a chance to talk out the *situation*. Listen carefully, empathize, feed back, and then say, "Okay, I hear what you're saying. What can you do about it?" Help her explore the *options* (none are too far out). Many people get stuck in decision making because they see only one option or none. Help your child learn to think of many different ways she could respond to the given situation.

The next step becomes more complex in that you want him to look at possible *consequences,* both negative and positive, of each option. This helps him think through the situation rather than just react to his dilemma. Children need to learn that choices have consequences. It's like choosing a path in the woods. Some consequences may be negative, some positive, and some just different. They also need to learn that they cannot always fully estimate the result of their decision. Like unexplored trails in the woods, we may be surprised by the unexpected. Encourage children to make the best decision they can with the information they have. Help your child learn to pray for guidance, and then choose an option that leads to a *solution.* Learning to act on the decision made is the next and last step.

Finally, we want our children to learn that solutions based on the principles of Jesus may not focus on what's in it for them or on immediate gratification, but rather what's best and right. Help children see the difference. Remember that if we guide them through the process of value decision making, they may not always come up with our answers, but they're developing an inner resource that says "Slowly I am learning how to make the best decisions I can. It's my decision and I'm responsible for it." They need this ability to help them make a conscious decision to follow Jesus Christ. The Christian life entails many critical choices necessitated by moral, spiritual, and ethical questions.

Travel tips

Now you're on your way. You have chosen the river road. As you ease your way down the steep descent, reflect on these tips for building self-esteem in your child. Self-esteem is one of God's good ideas.

1. Affirm your child when things go well, but don't reject her if she misbehaves. Learn to reassure her, but also share your feelings about her behavior. Talking it out can lead to healing. If you contributed to the problem, acknowledge that and ask your child's forgiveness.

2. Hear your child out before you make a rash judgment about incidents that arise. Give him a chance to talk it out, and treat him with respect. Explore optional ways of resolving a problem or behavior.

3. Establish reasonable expectations. Encourage her to do her best, but make it clear that perfection is not expected. Your child has to know that she is accepted even when she fails.

4. Let your child know that his feelings are important to you. Listen when he wants to talk. Don't moralize or lecture. Provide comfort and support when needed.

5. Don't compare your child with siblings or others her age. Treat her as a unique being with particular abilities, per-

sonality, and interests. Touch base with her where she is rather than where you want her to be.

For review and response

Recap

1. Our children are growing up in a nuclear century, a space age, a technological era, moving onto an information highway that will radically alter the way people relate and think.

2. Every day our children face inner and outer conflicts, wants, desires, and temptations, sometimes with few tools available for resolving them. The rights and wrongs that were once quite clear have become rather murky. Even parents get fuzzy about how to resolve some of the issues.

3. We empower our children by building their self-esteem. Confident children who feel good about themselves will be able to make better decisions than those who experience life otherwise.

4. Values reinforced by self-esteem undergird good decisions.

5. By assessing your own values, you are empowered to communicate these beliefs to your child in a consistent manner.

6. If we guide our children through the process of value decision making, we establish a basis for following Jesus Christ.

What then shall we do?

1. Think back to your childhood. Identify times you felt bad about yourself. How were these feelings resolved? Who affirmed your worth?

2. Evaluate your decision-making processes. Do you make impulsive decisions? avoid decisions? look at options?

How does your decision-making process affect your life in Christ and ways you share your faith?

    3. Give your children allowances (see chapter 11, page 188). Some of the allowance should not be designated for specific items. Freedom to plan and spend facilitates decision making. Guide children as needed. Don't bail them out if they run short of money. Identify other practical decision-making areas.

For family

Family time

    1. *Family faith stories.* Telling your story and those of previous generations creates a family identity, helps your children learn about the values upheld, and tells them about the faith life of their predecessors. Explore your family history and show photos, slides, movies, or videos. Invite members of your extended family to participate. Designate a time for this sharing, but don't rule out spontaneous storytelling while traveling, walking, working together, after meals, or before bedtime.

    2. *What would you do?* Children often must make difficult decisions. Introduce a dilemma (newspapers, books, real life incidents provide resources). Everyone has input. (Parents go last so they don't influence the children's responses.) Listen intensely, don't negate your child's response, and ask further questions to help him see the consequences of his decisions.

    3. *Games we play.* Playing games brings a family together if the focus is on fun rather than competition. Parents must model this. A freeing environment underlies natural sharing of your faith and your children's questions about God, and the like, at another time. Many games such as Chinese Checkers, Checkers, Chess, Bazaar, or Outdoor Survival also help your children develop decision-making skills. Look

for others in toy and game stores.

4. *What if?* Stretch your children's imaginations with activities that help them learn to explore options. Note that God must have a wonderful imagination to create a universe, earth, and humans in such infinite variety. Play a game. Someone asks a "what if" question, such as "What if oranges were long and bananas round?" "What if God created the world square?" "What if there were no Bible?" "What if all people lived underground?" Count the responses, then point to another person to ask a question. Have fun.

5. *I heard good news.* Share the story of your decision to become a follower of Jesus. Doing so frees your children to ask questions and seek counsel. Also share the good news by reading aloud to your children. Select books like Lehn's *I Heard Good News Today* (Faith & Life Press, 1983). During younger years, children will enjoy the well-told stories. Older children ready to emulate heroes may think of these characters as models for faith. Provide good news materials and resources, but never push or manipulate your child into making a decision. Faith and a faith decision are the work of the prompter, God's Spirit.

Celebrate the family

Celebrate the resurrection. Celebrate Easter by making Cross Cookies with your children. Mix a sugar cookie dough, chill, and roll into ropes. Cut into an equal number of lengths of four and two inches. Lay the shorter over the longer to form a cross, press down, sprinkle with colored sugar, and bake. As you eat them, note that the cross is empty. Jesus is alive. After eating, celebrate the resurrection. Divide the family into two groups. One loudly proclaims, "Christ is risen!" The other replies, "Christ is risen indeed!"

An idea for a family night activity

Church year centerpieces. Learn about events such as Advent, Christmas, Epiphany, or Pentecost by engaging in a family night activity. Adapt the following Easter idea: Read John 20:1-16. Discuss the event with your children and how you will build a scene. Create a garden scene on a place mat to serve as a centerpiece for your Easter dinner. Simple figures may be made by cutting four-inch lengths from large dowels and painting them or by gluing small plastic foam balls onto empty toilet-paper rolls, painting on features, and dressing them. Young children may add the grasses, twigs potted in modeling clay for trees, or early flowers arranged in baby food jars.

For study

Search the Scriptures

"Love must be sincere. Hate what is evil; cling to what is good" (Romans 12:9).

Romans 12:9-21 presents guidelines for Christian living—basic values and principles as guides for the Christian life. How are these like or unlike Jesus' principles listed in the Sermon on the Mount, Matthew 5—7?

How could these guidelines help you establish a value system from which to make decisions?

Discuss the questions

1. In what ways are our children facing a more complex world than we were at their age?

2. What are the most important decisions you want your child to make? How can good decision-making processes help your child in his or her faith development?

Engage in group response

1. Think of an incident when someone lowered your self-esteem. Share the story with your group. Discuss how this situation could have been handled differently. Choose group members to help role play the incident and create a positive ending. When finished, ask other members to respond.

2. What are ten values you would like to pass on to your children? Write these on a sheet of paper and share with the group. Commit yourself to reviewing these once a week.

3. What is the most difficult decision you ever made? Divide a sheet of paper in half. With crayons, doodle the incident and your feelings at the time. Share with the group.

Chapter 7

River Crossing

*Dealing with Individual and Family
Transitions*

A new path

The river road was less frightening than anticipated, but you couldn't know that. When we choose a direction, we can only anticipate what the journey will be like. This has been a good choice. You splashed and waded in low waters with your children and joined their merry laughter. Now it's time to go. You don't have to go back up the steep hill. On the other side, the path continues along a gentle slope. Near the bridge to your left, the water is shallow, and large flat boulders provide stepping-stones for crossing over. Hold your children's hands firmly and guide them over the wet, slippery rocks. Before you cross, let me tell you what an Alaskan ranger told our family: "River crossings can be dangerous. It is better not to attempt them alone. Hold hands in shallow water. When the water is deep and swift, make a human chain tied together with strong ropes. That way no one gets swept away."

Crossing the river not only leads you to the other side but also brings you to a different environment and a new path. River crossings are not unlike the transitions we and our children go through. The word "transition" has taken on new meaning in today's world of rapid shifts and changes. Several decades ago, life was simpler and slower. Today it is fast, more intense, and filled with change. Urbanites may especially feel not only the pace but also the loneliness and isolation induced by mobility. My husband and I live in a newer community, primarily families from all over the United States and some from other countries. I sense the loneliness of many who have left friends or family because of job change or transfer.

There are other shifts in our society. Technology revolutionizes our way of life. The information highway, heavily loaded with present and future possibilities, changes the way we think. We can't avoid it; if we don't get on board, we may feel as if a train is passing by and we've been left behind. Life in the fast lane places high demands on us and our children. Change makes constant transitions necessary for all family members.

Transitions can be productive in the long run. When dealt with positively, change produces new options, growth, and maturity. It may also produce insecurity, loneliness, and anxiety. During a time of change, we are compelled to share a faith with our children that professes God as refuge (Psalm 16:1), shepherd (23:1), light (27:1), strength (46:1), and much more. It is as important to support and strengthen the sense of family and extended family as it is to hold hands and cling to each other during a river crossing.

In today's world, we engage in so many crossings that many of us may feel our feet are constantly wet. Our questions about transitions and sharing faith with our children who are a part of these transitions are rooted in the changes we are experiencing.

What are transitions and how do they affect us?

Transition is change that affects you or your children directly. The events of our lives, whether planned or unplanned, continue to present us with change. What we often don't realize is how that change affects us and our children. A transition moves us from where we've been to a new place. Sometimes, like the shallow river crossing you made, the passage is relatively simple and we eagerly look forward to exploring what's on the other side. At other times, rushing flood waters create dangerous undertows. We cling to each other, barely able to survive. Unlike a river crossing, however, a transition is a one-way street. We can't go back.

Transition means that we say good-bye to one way of being, thinking, or living and hello to a new experience. But we can't just jump from one side to the other. River crossings take time. Grief is involved in change, and we find ourselves in an in-between stage of limbo where we may feel confused and unsure or depressed and sad. It is important to say good-bye well, to recognize the good things about the past, or to make peace with past hurting events or relationships. Unless we come to grips with that and help our children talk out their feelings, we will have a hard time moving forward and growing through the change.

The in-between time during transition may be accompanied by feelings of dis-ease, anxiety, or lostness. If it's a painful change, the seething river crossing may take much longer. During difficult times, you need to seek help and support for yourself and your children. Doing it alone or even as a couple is too frightening and isolating. Wild river crossings are dangerous. The ropes are like the support you lend each other within the immediate family, but also the strength of extended family willing to cross over and walk with you.

During times of change, empower your children with your ongoing trust in God. During difficult transitions, there may be times when that trust wavers. Don't feel guilty. Believe that the Great Presence will heal. Remember, God weeps with you when you suffer. Through this turbulent river crossing, this stressful shift, believe that God is holding both you and your children's hands, even when you're letting go. The Sustainer of all life and hope will never loosen the divine handclasp.

Transitions inevitably create stress. Be aware that if a number of transitions occur at one time, the stress may be compounded. For example, if you are going through divorce, your children have to develop a new way to relate to their parents. Former family friends may distance themselves or even take sides. Change in financial status may force you to change homes, take on another job, or adjust to a new neighborhood. These stressors are not isolated from each other; they are events that pile up, each weighing the other down more heavily. When stressful events compound, coping ability goes down. You or your child may explode over minor incidents, even if you're able to cope with major changes. At a certain point, stress, if not dealt with, may lead to illness or family problems. Children, especially young ones, tend to act out their bewilderment or to withdraw. Talking things out, taking time for each one, assuring them, and supporting them will be much more helpful than punishment during times when their behavior is an expression of inner confusion.

Transitions, particularly difficult ones, take time. You and your children are crossing a river, not a puddle. Too often, we try to shortcut this period. If you have moved and your child doesn't like the school, you may placate her and say, "It'll be okay soon," or maybe even tell her she shouldn't feel that way. If we've experienced divorce, the painful process may cause us to jump into another marriage. In either of these situations, we are limiting the potential for growth, of gaining a deeper insight and understanding of ourselves and God in this given situation.

Transitions affect everyone in the family. Children have an uncanny ability to know what's going on around them, even when parents try to hide their feelings. A child going through the moods and irritabilities of transition may not be able to identify what's happening, but the behaviors and attitudes create a chain reaction. One suffers; all suffer. Someone has said that a family is like a canoe filled with people. Every time someone moves or leaves, all others are affected as they try to adjust to the change. During change, it is important for families to repeatedly verbalize the fact that they are *for,* not *against,* each other. Help your children trust in a God who gives us the ability to choose, think, and feel. Even when it hurts, God is there to help us make decisions that will move us across the river to the welcoming banks on the other side.

Can we get along without transitions?

Transitions are a part of life. Even on a desert island, you can't control the changes taking place around and in you. Many biblical stories tell of transitions that changed an individual's or a group's life. The flood, the exodus from Egypt, and the exile in Babylon are major ones. The grumbling of the exodus people (Exodus 14:11, 16:3) and the weeping of the exiles (Psalm 137:1) are indications of how these people were affected by their changes. How do you think Rebekah felt when she left her homeland to become Isaac's wife? What kind of transition did King Saul go through when David's popularity threatened his throne? How did Peter's call to be Jesus' follower change his family? What kind of transitions did the young church go through when persecution set in? There are many more.

Transitions occur persistently. Many are so minor or taken for granted that we don't recognize them as such. Years ago I attended a family workshop led by Margaret Sawin. Through role play, we identified stages of change in a family's life. Children were tied to the parents and to each other. Incidents like a first day of school, buying new clothes, and a birthday party created tugging in this family web. When a new baby was added, all members were tugged in that direction. These are the common transitions. Think of how this web shudders and shakes if crises occur.

We can't get along without transitions. God is a God of change, transition, and creativity. Out of that comes growth. Divine power makes all things new, again and again. We do well to teach our children that change is a part of our life under God. We need to support them during their transitions, encourage them to talk out their feelings, help them understand what is happening, and patiently walk with them through the river. Become aware of how your child's transition is also affecting you. This can make you more sensitive to meeting your child's emotional and spiritual needs. During critical times, try to establish a serene, quieter mood at home. Cut back on activities, simplify your lifestyle, play family games, and take time to think and talk about your past experiences. Cross the river, then sit on the bank for a while. Rest and let the afternoon sun warm you. Let your children know that the everlasting Son will help each one take the next step.

Are there different kinds of transitions?

I divide transitions into four categories—*normal life, chosen, forced,* and *transitions of the mind.* None of these is the same for any one child or parent because the environment and situation in which they occur varies from one individual to another.

Normal transitions. In chapters 3–5, we discussed the developmental stages of children and the disequilibrium experienced during each phase of growth. Growth stages are transitions in your child's life. Normal transition is one of God's good ideas. We need to understand these stages to keep us from seeing our child as a behavior problem, rather than one who is engaged in a river crossing. This doesn't mean a laissez faire attitude on a parent's part. But in gripping the child's hand, encouraging her to share and talk, understanding what's happening and sharing your faith, you guide your child through a transition towards greater maturity.

One of the difficult phases an older child faces is the loss of childhood; the world of wonder and awe becomes superseded by reality. I remember the day I walked into my playhouse in the trees where logs had served as couches and broken pieces of glass as elegant china. My imagination had always magically transformed that world into something beautiful. Now I suddenly saw it for what it was. Sadness stole over me. No matter how much I tried to wish it back, it wouldn't come.

Chosen transitions. We tend to think of transitions as problem related. But many of the changes which also create stress in our lives occur during times when all is well and we choose our new challenges. We may fail to identify or talk about feelings we have about the change because we are supposed to be happy. Choosing marriage is a river crossing. Two individuals leave a particular lifestyle and try to forge one that is compatible to both.

Another transition is the birth of the first baby. Again, according to baby showers and cards, babies are a bundle of joy. But who has warned parents about the dynamics that take place when two become three? New parents don't get enough sleep, their focus is on an infant who demands their time, and routine is broken. A young mother said, "I'm so depressed. I haven't even had time to take a bath." But to whom can you talk about your mixed feelings without feeling guilty? You're in transition.

Chosen transitions come in many shapes and sizes. Visualize your child's first day at school. I remember the tears in my eyes when our six-year-old boarded the bus. An old chapter was ending and a new one, beginning. Whether you choose to move, buy a new house, accept a better job, or your child makes new choices, all affect the family.

Unchosen transitions. Many transitions in the lives of parents and family feel like struggles against wild river rapids. You lose your job, or to keep your job, you're expected to transfer to another state. Mobility continues to be one of the great stressors in modern society. A psychologist has said it's like pulling a rosebush up by the roots and transplanting it. If you identify the transplanting as a transition, you and your children will be less likely to displace your anger and frustration onto each other. This may be a good time to talk about some of the stories in the Bible that tell of transitions and change. David left home to become king. Paul's job was to share the gospel, but he ended up in jail. Talk about ways biblical characters did or did not handle their transitions well. Then discuss what you as a family team can do to make this time of change as manageable as possible.

Tragic unchosen transitions are the most difficult to cope with. These are not God's good ideas, but they happen. Families are devastated by wars, revolution, and violence. Closer to home, unsuspecting families are shattered by tragic events that make them feel as though they will not be able to cross this roaring river. How can your faith hold together when your world is falling apart? when someone in your family is diagnosed with a terminal or debilitating illness? when a spouse or child becomes disfigured or disabled through accident? when spouse or child are diagnosed with a mental illness? when your child is the victim of violence or abuse? when your spouse walks out on you or dies?

Many other crises create unwelcome transitions. Your awareness of how you and your children are being affected, even at times when you feel empty and confused, may keep you focused when it appears the whole family is becoming disfunctional. God's grace will never let you go. Make a prayer that you say together each day. Assure your children. Even if you only say the words, someday you will live in hope again. Believe that at some point in the future your feet will touch dry ground.

Transitions of the mind. Paul indicates that we are to have the mind of Christ (1 Corinthians 2:16b). But changing one's attitudes and ways of thinking involves a transition that affects our lives and those of our children. Sometimes it takes a crisis to catapult us into more open-minded thinking or into a new level of faith. In Acts 10, Peter is shocked by a vision from God that forces him to believe that the gospel is for Gentiles as well as Jews. You may not have to deal with your racial prejudice until a family moves in next door. You may not deal with your judging attitudes and narrow view of religion until a crisis in your life makes you cry for empathy and understanding from others. You may not have to deal with your homophobia or sexist attitudes until your boss hires an assistant manager who is a lesbian parenting two children. Your children face similar issues today and may mirror your prejudices. Prejudice runs rampant in schools. Words like "fag" and "nigger" are used by youngsters who don't know what they mean. In small, closed communities, any new child may feel unaccepted because she doesn't "fit." Children are not naturally prejudiced. They mimic what they are exposed to at home, school, in the neighborhood, and through the media.

Think of Jesus as your model for empathy, compassion, and acceptance. Let the divine Spirit identify your areas of prejudice and closed-mindedness. Only when you understand yourself will you be able to help your children deal with the prejudices that build walls, not bridges.

Travel tips

Crossing over and reflecting on the riverbank have given you much to think about. As you look at the transitions in your family and pray for present and future guidance, consider these tips:

1. Your family's life under God is not static; it is constant movement toward greater maturity, marked by transitions. Transitions—especially difficult ones—can't be rushed. Identify ways to release the past before you greet your new experiences, and help your children to do the same.

2. Transitions create stress which affects you and your children. Develop stress coping skills for the whole family, such as exercise, relaxing techniques, family together times, talking it out, memory sharing, and humor. Singing, listening to soothing music, praying together, and sharing stories also help you deal with stress. Try to maintain family routines or rituals.

3. Recognizing a transition keeps you from believing the problem is unsurmountable or permanent. Help your children realize that it's okay to feel confused, sad, or anxious. Guide them through changes with questions, such as "What can we do about this? What are ways we can be there for each other?" Share with them that God is always there, through good and difficult days.

For review and response

Recap

1. The word "transition" has taken on new meaning in today's world of rapid shifts and changes.

2. Transition is change that affects you or your children directly. The events of our lives, whether planned or unplanned, continue to present us with change. A transition moves us from where we've been to a new place.

3. Grief is involved in change. We find ourselves in an in-between stage of limbo where we may feel confused, unsure, depressed, or sad.

4. Transitions, particularly difficult ones, take time. When stressful events compound, coping ability goes down.

5. Transitions occur persistently in the daily lives of parents and children. They affect everyone in the family.

6. Transitions may be divided into four categories: normal, chosen, unchosen, and transitions of the mind.

7. Your family's life under God is not static; it is constant movement toward greater maturity, marked by transitions.

What then shall we do?

1. Identify transitions you have gone through during each decade of your life. Write them down. How did you handle them? Do you perceive a pattern in how you deal with change? Where did your trust in God fit in?

2. Reflect on transitions your children have gone through. Identify a change your child is experiencing presently. How does this chapter help you understand (stand under) and support him or her?

3. My grandfather, migrating from Russia to Canada in 1925, kept a diary aboard ship. When wind and waves were

high, he quoted Isaiah 43:2 in his daily entry, a river crossing affirmation. Read it and make this your personal trust word for difficult times.

For family

Family time

1. *"Spin the Bottle" for fun.* Humor is a great healer and relationship builder. Laughter is God's gift to us. Find a bottle, sit in a circle on the floor, and ask a child to start the game by spinning the bottle. When the bottle stops and the neck points to someone, that child or parent tells a joke, a funny story, or a humorous incident that happened recently. When finished, he or she spins the bottle, and it becomes someone else's turn to bring laughter to the family.

2. *Height marks.* Tape a five-foot length of paper on the wall. Measure each child's height and make a black mark on the paper. Use a red crayon to mark in the number of inches each one measured at birth. Talk about change and growth. Ask them what they can do now that they couldn't do when they were "red-mark people." Discuss other changes your family has gone through, such as moving, different schools, new brother or sister, leaving friends, and others. Ask: "What is it like now?" Commend your children for handling their changes to the best of their ability. (Single parent and blended families may want to deal with questions related to their situations.) Let them know that God is there to help. Share your faith by affirming that growth is God's good idea, and change, even if difficult, helps us grow in different ways.

3. *Rhythmic chant.* A rhythmic chant is a word or series of words repeated to clear your mind, relax, and assure you. During a time of transition in your family, talk about the changes and some of the concerns or worries these may bring.

Encourage children to share their feelings. Explain a rhythmic chant, and learn the following words of assurance from Hebrews 13:6 (as you repeat these words, emphasize the underlined words): "The <u>Lord</u> is my <u>helper</u>; I will <u>not</u> be <u>afraid</u>."

4. *Make puppets.* Simple puppets can be used to tell Bible stories or family stories. They may also be used informally to talk out feelings. Children often find it easier to communicate this way. Decide together what you will do. If someone is undergoing change, tell the story with puppets. This provides a natural, casual way to share your faith through the mouth of your character.

Here are three simple puppets you can make: (1) Draw or cut a figure from a magazine, back with heavy paper, and staple onto a rod or stick. Move the characters by holding the sticks. (2) With markers, draw a face on the bottom of a closed brown lunch sack. Extend the mouth to the side of the sack so that when you put your hand in the sack, you can move the mouth. (3) Cut two 1 1/2-inch/3.75-centimeter circles from white felt. Glue a black paper or cloth 1/2-inch/1.25-centimeter circle onto the middle. Double up and fasten masking tape to the back. Use as eyes on any item, such as a bottle, tennis shoe, glass, etc. For a fun time, all might want to choose an item that best characterizes them and see what kind of story they could come up with.

5. *First-day friends.* Share how Jesus cared about, had compassion for, and was a friend to those who needed him. Share your faith and help your children share theirs by being a cheerleader or booster for someone who is going through a "first." These firsts may be celebrative or difficult, giving your children opportunity to share either joy or compassion. Think of special people who are going through a first in their lives, like a first day in school, hospitalization, death of a pet or family member, or the birth of a new brother or sister. Make your

children aware of adult transitions—firsts such as retirement, a new job, graduation, wedding, leaving home, divorce, loss, new baby, etc. Plan to do something special for someone in transition, whether it's a joyful or painful first. Ideas: letters or notes, visits, homemade cards or gifts, baked cookies, or a family coupon booklet in which you offer free items or services to the recipient. Think of others.

Celebrate the family

Celebrate Advent. Celebrate Advent with candlelighting, reading, singing, and a nativity scene. (Make a simple board by drilling five holes for candles into a piece of wood, or pushing four red candles into a thick styrofoam circle and one white one into the middle. Cover the base with real or artificial greens.) Each Sunday a child lights one of the candles. Read a segment from the nativity story (such as pages 102-109 from Lehn's *God Keeps His Promises*) and sing a carol. If you have a nativity scene, place the figures at a distance from the manger; each Sunday have children move them closer. (Keep the infant hidden.) On Christmas eve or morning, children light the white Christ candle and arrange all the figures around the manger. Bring out the Christ child and ask someone to place it in the manger.

An idea for a family night activity

Hobby night. Hobbies develop skills and interests. They are particularly helpful during times of stress and change. If your children don't have hobbies, bring ideas or hobby articles to a family night to discuss some options, and get started. Hear the children's ideas. Help them select hobbies that are suitable for their age. Provide crayons and newsprint for those who are not old enough to start a hobby.

For study

Search the Scriptures

"How can we sing the songs of the Lord while in a foreign land?" (Psalm 137:4).

In 586 B.C. the armies of Nebuchadnezzar destroyed Jerusalem and exiled the people to Babylon. Read Psalm 137 and note the depression caused by this major transition. Identify words in the passage that indicate how the people felt. What was the significance of hanging their harps on the willow trees? Why did they feel distanced from the Lord and unable to sing?

Discuss the questions

1. Using your Bibles, identify various transitions recorded in the testaments. Step into the characters' shoes and talk about how they may have felt.

2. What are the four major types of transitions? How does each type affect one's life? Where does faith come in?

Engage in group response

1. Write down on a sheet of paper those transitions you wish for your children. On the back, list those from which you wish your children could be spared. Share what you have written.

2. Draw two symbols to represent the most joyful and most painful transitions you or your family have experienced. Ask each other questions about how you dealt with these experiences.

3. As a group, design a family board game called *Transitions,* where dice are thrown for moving, and transition instructions along the way make the player go back, forward, wait a turn, etc. Add other ideas. Make a sign-up sheet and take turns checking it out and playing it at home.

Chapter 8

Listen to the Birds

Personalities of Children and Communication

....

What variety!

A re you and your children enjoying the walk? I hope you saw the purple wood violets and the shaded, late-blooming raspberries. Look closely and you'll see innumerable green plants, flowering shrubs, and fungi growing under trees, logs, and in sunlit spaces. Encourage your children to discover the wonderful diversity of God's nature. Stop for lunch under the tall pine near the path and rest on the thick, brown and green needle bed. Before you eat, thank God, and take a few moments to listen to the forest sounds around you.

God's variety in nature comes to us in what we hear and observe. Listen to the sounds of flying insects like butterflies, bees, and dragonflies. Observe the behavior of the crawlers and creepers like ants, spiders, and caterpillars. How about the birds? Do we know what they're up to? The seclusion of this tree near an open, grassy knoll gives you a fine spot from which to listen and watch as you eat.

Did you hear it? the knock-knock sound above you? Look up and you'll see a yellow-shafted flicker. His strong, sharp bill is drumming against the trunk, digging for insects. His stiff tail props him against the tree. You won't hear him now, but his song makes a flickering sound.

Look farther up. Resting quietly on a big branch sits a great horned owl. At twilight you'll hear her mournful hoots as she gets ready to do night hunting. Because of their large heads, owls are sometimes called wise. She's awake now and staring at us with her big, glassy eyes.

There are many other birds in and around woods, each with its own distinct colors, songs, and habits. You won't see them all, so continue your walk. Oh, just a moment; look back. There's a cavity on this side of the oak, a home of the green-backed tree swallow. Look quickly and you'll see one swoop down toward it. And look, there are several more nearby. Their long, pointed wings and forked tails make them elegant, graceful fliers.

You've reached a green, sun-filled opening. How unexpected! Sshh! Do you hear the whirring sound? It's a ruby-throated hummingbird, flashing in and out of the flowering bushes. Its rapid wing beat hums as it hovers above the blossom; inserts its long, slender bill; and daintily feeds on the nectar.

Awareness of God's beautiful world not only puts us and our children in touch with Genesis 1 and the incredible act of creation but also makes us aware that we are a part of that very act. God's intense creative nature demands more infinite variety than our minds can grasp. We respect variety in nature, but we appear to be less open to that same variety within the human race. Our insecurities demand sameness. They keep us from exulting in the wonder of those who are not like us.

There seems to be a pressure on the human mind, foreign to God's creative way of thinking, that cries for everyone to act and be the same. Many parents relate to each of their children in the same way, discipline them in the same manner, and expect the same responses. Through coercion, some parents may get the response and behavior they want with little consideration for the child's personality and particular needs. Learning about development stages may even lead us to think of each age-group behaving and responding in a certain manner. Remember, stages are only guidelines to give you a general understanding of the young one's growth and development patterns. Each child will develop at his or her own rate, affected by many other factors, including his or her unique personality. This thought raises questions for us to look at.

What is personality?

Our personality is God-given. It is us. Carl Jung, the psychologist, discovered a number of decades ago that his clients responded in a variety of ways, and he began to classify these responses and perceptions. He ended up with sixteen personality types, which are indicative of our preferences for how we function. These types were based on preferences in four areas: (1) Are we more *introverted* [I], tending to choose solitude or the inner world to become energized, or *extroverted* [E], tending to choose people or the outer world to become energized? (2) Do we think about things from the perspective of *sensation* [S], tending to choose a down-to-earth, factual, five senses approach to life, or *intuition* [N], inclined towards inspiration, imagination, and innovation? (3) Do we prefer to make decisions through *thinking* [T], selecting an impersonal, objective rational process, or *feeling* [F], a more subjective, personal, and people-oriented approach? (4) Do we settle things by *judging* [J], making decisions now, planning ahead, and seeking closure, or through *perceiving* [P], remaining flexible and tentative until all options are considered? (Isabel Briggs Meyers, *Gifts Differing,* Consulting Psychologists Press, 1980).

Individuals prefer one or the other in these four areas, and if you mix the preferences in different ways, you end up with a variety of ways of functioning. Each personality type perceives the world from a particular perspective. No one type is better than another; they're just different. For a better understanding of yourself and your significant others, I suggest you read Keirsey and Bates' *Please Understand Me* (Prometheus Nemesis Books, 1978).

No person is 100 percent inclined toward one preference or the other, but each of us has an innate preference stronger than its opposite that begins to emerge at or even before birth and *develops with time.* We may use the opposite but always feel more comfortable in our natural preference.

Why do we need to discuss and learn about personalities?

By recognizing variants in personality, you can begin to identify these God-given attributes in yourself and your children. This helps you understand and affirm the different ways you and your children relate to each other and encounter the world around you. It will also help you to understand how you can most effectively communicate your faith to each of your children. Various personalities worship, pray, and experience God differently. Understanding a personality, however, does not mean you label your child or put her in a box. Your child is not an object. Understanding means to become aware, to act with compassion, to be sensitive to, to "stand under" (understand), but not to categorize or even excuse certain behaviors.

In marriage or family, we readily assume others should

be, think, feel, and function like us. For example, two people marry, delighting in their oppositeness. Unconsciously, opposites attract each other. Not long after the wedding, however, the discomfort of the opposite leads to criticism. Each one tries to make the other over to be like him or her. Instead of understanding the oppositeness as a creative possibility for stretching and growing together, they begin to whittle away at each other. The more opposite they are, the greater the urge to sculpt the other into an image of one's liking. The very things that drew a couple together become the basis for dissension.

The same thing happens with our children. Even though we looked at the developmental tasks and faith stages of children, this does not mean children are all the same. They're not cut out with cookie cutters. The stages of development in all areas remain consistent, but they are experienced and expressed in a variety of ways by the young ones God has given us to nurture, care for, and share our faith with. When our personality preference clashes with that of our child, we may express that difference through criticism, and the child is made to feel she doesn't measure up. Instead of nurturing the child's preference, we may urge her to act and think primarily in ways that are familiar to us but foreign to her being. Or, in some cases, when the nurturing parent's personality is opposite to that of the child, he or she will unconsciously and lovingly socialize that child at an early age to perceive and act like the parent, because that's what that parent is most comfortable with. It is valuable for a child to learn opposite tasks, but not at the expense of retarding the development of his or her personality.

What are some personality clues that will help me understand my child?

We cannot address all types in this chapter, but we want to look at four temperaments who express, relate to, and experience life in different ways. These are only hints, because other dynamics such as extroversion, introversion, or how decisions are made (let alone environmental and age factors) all affect how individuals express themselves. But the basics of temperaments are represented in the following. I will introduce the characteristics of these temperaments by using names of the birds you saw in the green woods a short time ago, making it easier to understand and more fun for your older children.

Yellow-shafted flickers [SJ] are factual, orderly, and dependable. Family and extended family are important. Flickers find change unsettling and have difficulty perceiving options. They want to belong and contribute, but preferably in familiar surroundings. They need to be appreciated for their work. Young flickers (children) enjoy routine, step-by-step instructions, crafts, factual stories and pictures, and fill-in-the-blank types of activities. They relish rewards. They are obedient and like to please. They are the only one of the four temperaments who respond well to physical punishment or criticism and make behavior changes accordingly. Young flickers are frustrated when they're to come up with ideas, are confused by numerous options, feel threatened by change, and are competitive. They need encouragement and appreciation for tasks well done.

Green-backed tree swallows [NF] look for meaning and authenticity. Significant relationships are central. Swallows focus on ideas, possibilities, and self-actualization through intuitive vocations. They crave ideal relationships. Conflict creates high anxiety. They need appreciation for who they are rather than for what they do. Young swallows (children) thrive on imaginative stories, use fantasy in play, and feel nourished through interaction with others. They like variety and freedom to make choices. Young swallows are sensitive, easily hurt by criticism, rejection, or broken promises. They are cooperative rather than competitive. Physical punishment devastates them. They need to have physical warmth and love shown by the parents.

Great horned owls [NT] hunger for knowledge and new ideas, especially about theories and technology. Owls want to control reality, are self-critical, and crave competency and knowledge. Communication is objective and logical, and they may miss emotional messages. Owls may be accused of being impersonal, but have deep inner feelings. They need to be treated fairly. Young owls (children) are independent and idea-oriented. They're obedient in things to which they're indifferent, but unyielding in issues that matter to them. They are offended by criticism or physical punishment. Young owls don't show affection readily, but do have emotional needs. They need to feel accepted, be treated with respect, be helped when they ask for help, and be listened to. They want to be appreciated for the quality of their work.

Ruby-throated hummingbirds [SP] focus on action, freedom, and spontaneity. They live in the present. Hummingbirds spend freely, like excitement, and are impulsive. They are fun-loving, yet durable; they survive setbacks and deprivations better than any other type. They feel confined if they have to wait or plan ahead. They are loyal and willing to share. Young hummingbirds (children) are good-humored and want immediate gratification. Because of short concentration, they need frequent change and excitement. Impulsive behavior may get them into frequent jams which don't rattle them. They like drama, games, competition, and contests. Hummingbirds rarely pay attention to directions and are indifferent to scolding or physical punishment. They're good team players, and you may get their cooperation by working together. They want to be appreciated for their performance.

How do personality differences or similarities affect relationships?

Differences in personality cannot be clearly distinguished in early years, because all young children are concrete in their thinking. But you can get some early clues. If you're in public and your baby watches and smiles at people, she's probably a swallow. If your two-year-old is super active, he may be a hummingbird. When our two-year-old called a flyswatter a butterfly bat and developed an imaginary friend at age four, I recognized a swallow.

Rarely will you have a family where each one is a different personality type, but you may have several represented. The intent of this chapter is to make you aware of that. If you and your spouse have the same personalities, you may have difficulty seeing options required for children who are different from you. If your focus in parenting is to conform (flicker), you may face difficulties with the active hummingbird or the independent owl or the imaginative swallow. If both your personalities are different, there is more possibility that one of you can relate better to one child than the other. The difficulties may come when you can't agree on a style of child rearing. The flicker child feels particularly unsettled when parents have different rules or ways of doing things.

One pitfall is that you may find yourself more at ease with a child closest to your personality type. It's easy to plan activities, worship experiences, and story time because you understand that child. It takes more work to plan for and understand the child who is different. Before you know it, you merely lay down the rules without listening to that child's needs. Your home will be enhanced if you are aware of the variety and treat each child as an individual. These are God-given traits. Thinking about ways to develop your relationship with each child can mean growth for you. Being aware of the differences helps you plan activities that will enrich the various personalities in your home. Each child learns best in his or her preferred style: a flicker in more question-answer style; a swallow in creative group experiences; an owl through research and idea sharing; and the hummingbird through active, hands-on projects. This doesn't mean children should be exposed only to their styles, but it makes you aware of the need to plan for more options and approaches.

Being aware of differences will also help you reflect on the spiritual guidance you give. Your flicker child enjoys memory work and looking up Bible verses. Your swallow child likes group sharing and holding hands while praying. Your owl child likes to reflect on thoughts about God. And your hummingbird will like service projects. Your flicker child may want to learn and repeat a prayer. Your swallow may prefer to make her own. Your owl may ask many questions but prefer to pray alone. Your hummingbird will need short prayer and devotion times before starting to squirm. It is quite probable that as you guide your children through the faith stages of trust, worth, and belonging, their different personalities may experience God in various ways.

How do personality differences or similarities affect communication?

Communication entails both talking and listening. We assume that the other understands us because we have talked, but that is not so. The more opposite you are from another's personality, the more difficult and energy-demanding communication becomes. It's important to concentrate and to double check to discover whether the other understood what you said and meant. If your personality is the same as your spouse's or child's, communication is so clear that you can almost read each other's minds. Remember that not everyone else perceives reality as you do.

When you begin to realize how complex communication is, you will want to find ways to improve that communication. The most critical element in sharing your faith with your child is to learn to listen for feedback. You cannot assume that what you have said is understood by your child. When you listen to your child, you need to sit down, have eye contact, and give her your wholehearted attention. Too often we act as if we're listening but our mind is actually preparing our next statement or defense. Children can soon tell whether we are genuine.

As you listen and become aware of your child's personality, you also need to learn to respond to that child in a way that makes sense to him or her. If you are a flicker parent, affirm the imaginative ideas about God that your swallow child has. Or if your owl child wants more than a traditional answer, suggest that you search together. A flicker parent and hummingbird child may have a hard time because these young ones won't conform and are readily labeled hyperactive. If you have one in your family, balance out the spiritual needs of all by also considering this young one. Act out the Bible stories rather than read them. Sing and make up action songs and involve your family in hands-on service and mission experiences. That is how faith will be best communicated to this active child. Owl parents may not always be aware of the feeling dynamics within a family; they need especially to learn listening techniques that validate the feelings of a swallow child. In this context and with this awareness, you can then better share your faith in a meaningful way. It is hard to enter into another's world, but I encourage you to prayerfully try, and the Great Listener will grace you.

Travel tips

We must hurry on because there are menacing clouds gathering in the west. I'm leaving one tip to help you think about your children in broader, more helpful ways as you continue to share your faith.

1. Our world, created by the Master Architect, contains an endless entourage in nature. A short time ago, you were exposed to the variety of flowers, insects, and birds in the woods. You saw, observed, and listened to the winged creatures. That same variety is evident among humans. God doesn't make clones. We and our children are sacred beings, each born with a temperament that develops into a personality that is uniquely ours. Granted, other factors such as biological makeup, culture, family environment, our placement within the sibling group, and the experiences we encounter influence us. But our innate preferences won't change. Our personalities are as unique to us as spots on a leopard. Differences in personality: one of the Eternal Creator's good ideas.

For review and reflection

Recap

1. God's intense creative nature demands more infinite variety than our minds can grasp.

2. There seems to be a pressure on the human mind, foreign to God's way of thinking, that cries for everyone to act and be the same.

3. Personality is God-given. It is us. God doesn't make clones. We and our children are sacred beings, born with a temperament that develops into a personality that is uniquely us.

4. When our personality preference clashes with that of our child, we may express that difference through criti-

cism. That child is made to feel that she or he doesn't measure up.

5. If you and your spouse have the same personalities, you may have difficulty seeing options required for children who are different from you.

6. Being aware of personality differences will also help you reflect on the spiritual guidance you give.

What then shall we do?

1. Don't put your child in a box or tell him "You are like this or this...." Rather, watch for signals in your child that better help you understand that particular individual's personality.

2. Remember that the more different your personality types, the more difficult your communication. Listen intensely to your child and try to respond from where she is, not from where you are. Helping your child flourish and grow is an act of creation.

3. Reflect on ways you can uniquely share your faith with each of your children. Provide various activities and experiences that help each child nurture his or her God-given personality and faith.

For family

Family time (activities for different temperaments)

1. *Musical appreciation.* Sit in a circle. Number each person, write the numbers on cards, mix them, and place upside down in the center of the circle. The starter puts a cap on, removes it, and passes it to the right while a leader plays or sings a song. The next one puts the cap on and passes it to the right. When the music stops, the one left holding the cap pulls

a number from the box. The cap holder must make a positive statement to the person whose number was picked, beginning with "What I like about you is _____." When done, the music continues. (Involve extended family, if possible.)

2. *Wildflower search.* Go to the park or to the country. Provide a wildflower identification book, camera, paper, and crayons. Search for wildflowers. Whoever finds one calls out, and all gather there. If someone finds it in the book, show it and read the information or place a marker in the book for later reference and discussion. Look at it closely and marvel at the intricacy and beauty of God's creation. Photograph or draw a picture of the flower. Once home, post your drawings on the wall.

3. *Truth about kindness.* Tell about Jesus' kindness, using short stories from the Gospels. Make a TRUE and FALSE sheet, listing what kindness is or is not. Call it KINDNESS IS.... Make copies and ask each family member to fill in the answers with a T or F. If your children are younger, you may want to do this together. Here are some examples: KINDNESS IS to play with a new kid and help her make friends. KINDNESS IS to hurt feelings and make others cry. KINDNESS IS to start an argument.

4. *Acts of kindness.* Read 1 Thessalonians 5:15. Divide into two groups. Group 1 is a Haitian family, and Group 2 is your family. Ask Group 2 to act out an ending to the following situation and Group 1 to respond accordingly: "A family from Haiti moved in next door, and certain neighbors are upset. Some don't like their dark skin. Others shout bad names at them. Last night someone threw eggs and tomatoes at their house. What will your family do?"

5. *Snowflakes.* Talk about how snow looks, feels, and tastes. Note that God is a God of variety, and no two snowflakes are alike. Make snowflakes. Cut white paper into

different-sized circles. Show your children how to fold them in half, quarters, eights, etc. Cut out shapes along the folded edges and at the top. Unfold and note how each person's snowflake is different. Use thread and tree ornament hooks to hang them. At Christmastime, make small ones to decorate your tree.

Celebrate the family

Celebrate "Around-the-World" Christmas. Enlarge your children's faith world by learning and experiencing how Christians in other countries celebrate Christmas. Here are a few thoughts: In England, carolers go from house to house sharing the good news in song. In France, families gather mosses, rocks, and more to build a nativity scene called a creche. In Sweden, the eldest daughter dresses in white and wears a crown of candles in remembrance of Lucia, a young Christian girl who refused to marry a pagan centuries ago and was martyred. She comes in and gives a Yuletide greeting; then she goes to each bedside with coffee and cinnamon buns. According to a story told about the reformer Martin Luther, in Germany, the green, lighted *tannenbaum* (Christmas tree) represents life and the starlit skies of that first Christmas. Which of these or others could you incorporate in your Christmas celebrations? For more ideas, as well as recipes for cookies and directions for ornaments from other countries, see my book *Christmas Everywhere* (Education Ministries, Inc., 1994).

An idea for a family night activity

Zoo visit. Celebrate the uniqueness of God's creation with a visit to the zoo. Draw your children's attention to the wide variety of animals, birds, fish, etc. If you have older children, plan a scavenger hunt. On a sheet of paper, list specific animals, birds, reptiles, etc., they are to find. Give a copy to each child. Each item listed merits two points. Those not listed earn one extra point each. The one with the most points may choose where the family will stop for a treat on the way home.

For study

Search the Scriptures

"There are different kinds of gifts, but the same Spirit" (1 Corinthians 12:4).

Paul corrects an error in the Corinthian church—that the main gift is that of speaking in tongues. He says there are as many gifts as there are body parts, and each has a part to play under the direction of the same Spirit. Read chapter 12, verses 12-30. What does Paul say about God's emphasis on variety?

List the gifts Paul mentions. Compare with Romans 12:6-8. These are not exhaustive lists, but only examples. What are your gifts? In what ways are they an expression of your particular personality type?

Discuss the questions

1. Why do we find it difficult to accept and relate to those among us in church and family who are different from us?

2. In what ways do we try to sculpt a spouse or child into our own image? What are possible consequences? possible options?

Engage in group response

1. If you or other group members have read *Please Understand Me*, recommended earlier, share the insights and understandings you have gained.

2. What makes worship meaningful for you? Share with the group and write your responses on a large sheet of newsprint. Discuss how personality differences in the family may affect how you plan and experience worship in your family.

3. In private devotions, including prayer, different personality types have dissimilar experiences. An SJ may engage in a regular devotion routine that makes him or her feel good. An NF may look for deeper meanings or even mystical experiences. An NT may feel drawn to God by a deep thought or insight. An SP may be uplifted by practical service or praying with others. Discuss your devotional and prayer experiences with each other. Reflect on how this may affect your family devotions at home.

Chapter 9

Thunder and Lightning

Helping Children Deal with
Crisis and Loss

Storm days

The clouds of early morning have piled up into huge, black thunderheads. The rumbling booms warn of a storm to come. Your frightened children cling to you. There is no time to lose. Lightning in the woods is dangerous. I suggest you follow the narrow path to your left. It leads to a trapper's winter hunting shack. You'll find shelter there. Go quickly. This dead, sultry quiet before the storm, with not a leaf stirring, indicates that rain or hail could pelt down any minute. There it is! Keep running. Safe at last, just in time. The storm is here. Wind roars through the treetops, hail bangs against the fragile windowpanes, lightning strikes, and thunder crashes. Who wouldn't be afraid? You can't change what's happening out there, but you can stick together and find comfort in one another's presence. Hold your children closely and sing some songs. Hugs make them feel secure, and your voices drown out the noise, momentarily diverting their attention.

There is much in life over which we have no control. The storms come and go, sometimes gusts and gales or thunderstorms, sometimes destructive tornadoes or hurricanes, and to the north, dangerous blizzards. During those times, one feels helpless, alone, and unprotected. These storms are not unlike the crises and subsequent feelings of loss and loneliness that we and our children experience throughout life. We wish and pray that our children could be protected from suffering and pain. But we have to recognize that they are as vulnerable as we in the face of the sudden, unexpected tempests that burst into unsuspecting lives.

Most of us go through life anticipating it will be good. We raise our children and share our faith in a loving God, even hoping that being Christian will insulate us from crisis, grief, and despair. We don't know what to do with Jesus' statement that the rain falls on the just and the unjust. We cannot understand how an almighty, loving God will let terrible things happen, especially to us. We know the Creator has endowed humanity with free will, but if that will constantly chooses evil, isn't it time for intervention? We know that terminal illness and deadly accidents are all around us, but somehow we assume those things happen to someone else. When they strike in our family, we begin to raise the "Why?" questions, because it just doesn't make sense. How can we cope with and help our children survive crisis? Is it even possible to share our faith during those difficult times? These may be only a few of the questions you are asking.

When is a crisis a crisis?

We must never underestimate the element of crisis in our child's life. Children have little experience on which to build, so minor events may appear catastrophic and final to them. Older children may be able to talk out their feelings and hurts, but the young are more prone to act out their misery. Be aware that what seems merely a bump in the grass to you may be a mountain to your child. Don't negate or minimize their heartbreaks. Comfort, console, and share your love and God's love with your children. It is important that you listen to your child and hear not only words but also the feelings behind the words.

Family crisis may be experienced differently by the young than by you, because of their self-centered, concrete thinking. Their world revolves around them and their needs. A classic example is a "Calvin and Hobbes" cartoon. The family returns from a wedding to find their home burglarized. The parents are overcome by fear and a sense of violation, but Calvin's only concern is to find his stuffed tiger. Once he finds Hobbes, he is comforted and the crisis is over, while the parents continue to be upset. The young are not ready to think of all the consequences related to a crisis. They need assurance and comfort and are ready to go on from there.

Not all parents experience crisis in the same way either. For some, a job loss is a catastrophe; for others, it is a challenge to try something new. For some, moving and leaving friends or family is a crisis; for others, it is a new opportunity. One reason for this may be the number of crises that have been experienced in the past year. Stress tends to accumulate. Another reason is a difference in personality. If you and your spouse experience crisis in a similar manner, the tension and stress may escalate. If you experience it differently,

one may give support to the other. Crises are especially difficult for a single parent. You have only yourself and your crisis
style to see you through. How easy to feel helpless and frightened. Don't go it alone. Reach out to extended family, a
dependable and trustworthy friend, or your pastor. They cannot resolve your problems, but can lend support in times of
pain and give another perspective if critical decisions need to
be made.

Maintaining one's faith in the midst of crisis may sometimes appear to be the only solid ground any parent's feet may
stand on. This doesn't mean you don't grieve or share feelings.
Not to do so is merely a suppression of feelings. But trust in
God, who gives you the ability to live with a spark of hope.
The Almighty will help you preserve a sense of serenity in the
midst of storms. This faith your children will see in you.

What are some of the crises our children face?

A transition of any kind involves loss. To gain something is also to lose something. At times the transition may be
experienced as crisis. Losing a precious object or a favored
toy may be felt intensely by your child, especially if that
object has been associated with comfort. We dare not underestimate how profoundly children feel the death of a beloved
pet. When eleven-year-old Bill's dog was hit by a car shortly
after the family moved to a new location, the two combined
events became a crisis for him. He lay on his bed for several
days, face to the wall, refusing to talk or eat.

Other crises in your child's life may involve rejection
by a friend or the loss of a friend due to a move. The average
family in the United States moves fourteen times during its life
span. Although these moves create possibilities for broad
experience, they also carry with them loss of relationships
and familiar surroundings. Even the very young feel this loss.

A mother said, "We moved when our son was eighteen months old and left behind our close friends and their one-year-old, Cory. They drove a VW bug, and our son called it 'Cory car.' Once unpacked, our family went for a drive, and when Aaron saw a VW, he called out excitedly, 'Cory car! Cory car!' A short time later, he noted a VW parked outside a home at the end of our street. Grabbing me by the hand, he insistently pulled me toward it, calling out, 'Cory car!' Young Aaron missed our friends as much as I did."

Other crises may involve prolonged illness or accident. Children have a hard time understanding why they have to remain in bed. Yet they develop an amazing tenacity. When six-year-old Byron fell, he broke both bones in one leg and was in a cast for two months. He felt isolated from summer fun and activity, but recouped by reading many books and inventing outdoor wheelchair games. Friends on bicycles soon joined him in this new sport.

Another potential crisis resides in the family shape. Although over 50 percent of North American homes are still two-parent homes, the remainder are single-parent and blended families (stepfamilies). Many of the homes today also have adopted children. Each of these experiences has the potential for crisis in the child's life. The adopted child facing identity issues during early adolescence may raise critical questions about why his parents gave him up. He may even be teased by others. The child in a single-parent home may face insensitive adults who ask about the other parent, sometimes with questions that cause the youngster to cringe. The blended family faces its own unique crisis potential, as each one has to give up something to adapt to a new relationship.

Lynn and Harry were both divorced. When they married each other, twelve-year-old Craig, who had assumed a protector role toward his mother earlier, felt usurped. He acted out the crisis of his lost role by nasty, rude behavior toward his stepfather. What should parents do? Crises like these require much prayer and wisdom by parents, because it's easier to punish the frustrated behaviors of children in crisis than to discover and deal with the causes.

We can't identify and discuss all the crises children face, but we hope our comments will help you understand your child when hard times come. Remember to view that crisis through your child's eyes. What you perceive as only a rainfall may for your child be a frightening thunderstorm.

What are the most critical crises a child faces?

Some crises which parents face are less critical to children because they are not directly involved. Yet they are affected. When a breadwinner loses a job and can't find a new one, when a parent or child is diagnosed with a mental illness, when accident or illness incapacitates a family member, or when a child is sexually abused or raped, all family members are affected. Crises like these rivet attention on the victim. The children not directly involved may feel alone, ignored, and even resentful. Some may feel guilty, thinking it should have happened to them, not to the other. Be aware of these needs for attention or inclusion. Maintain family rituals. Or, if you can't, call in extended family to help. Pray together with your children for the one hurt. Hold and hug them. Encourage talk times. Assure them that even if we can't understand why this happened, God is not letting go of us. If it helps, go through a pretend experience where each one holds out his or her hands and imagines God holding them tightly.

The most critical crises a child faces is that of divorce and parent or sibling death, because he or she is directly affected. Divorce changes the shape of the family, and children of all ages experience a sense of loss and grief in some way. Anger, hurt, anxiety, confusion, worry, and relief are some of the feelings a child may experience during divorce. Children may also feel guilt, thinking it was their fault.

Because the parents often suffer some of the same feelings as their children, they may at first be unable to meet the child's needs and thus are unaware of what these young ones are feeling. One woman said, "When John walked out, I was so devastated, I couldn't even cook. When someone dies, people bring in food and comfort, but when a relationship dies, you're given lectures and made to feel you must have done something wrong." During these times, children are sometimes left on their own emotionally, and they begin to act out their fears and anxieties. They are in crisis. Infants and toddlers may have temper tantrums, cling to the parent, or have trouble sleeping. The three- through five-year-olds may regress and become anxious and fretful. Early school-age children may feel sad, abandoned, and even rejected. They cry more and fantasize about bringing the parents back together. They become more disorganized and prone to impulsive behavior. Older children can better reason about what's happening, but may still exhibit anger, physical complaints, or become over-active to keep from dealing with what is happening.

Death is another major crisis for family members and again reshapes the family, but in a different way from divorce. In divorce there is often much anger, but in death there is sadness, depression, and loneliness. The loved one is gone, and no matter how much the child fantasizes about his or her return, those old enough to understand know it is final. Whether the death is that of a sibling, parent, or even the child's own death, each is a crisis to be dealt with. Some children find consolation in the thought of heaven, and others in the thought that Mommy or Daddy are still around, even if they can't be seen. The finality of death is hard for both children and adults to deal with. "I just wish I could see her," cried eleven-year-old Danny, tears streaming down his cheek. "I miss Mom so much."

Even the young feel the impact of death. A mother said, "When our nine-year-old was kidnapped and murdered, three-year-old Timmy wandered through the house, day after day, looking for his sister." A grandmother said, "When I was age seven, my mother died. I walked around for days, alone. I couldn't eat or play. I missed her so."

A child's own death may seem like a storm of hurricane proportions in the family. When the child is ill and knows she will die (Kubler Ross, in one of her lectures, maintained that children often know this long before the words have been said), you have to deal not only with your own pain but also the phases of grief your child is going through.

What are some ways to help children through divorce and death?

God does not want people to suffer, and we wish the Almighty One would divert life's agonies. We don't know how much accident and distress we are saved from each day. But we do know that the Bible is filled with stories of heartrending anguish and pain, with faith fluctuating between hopelessness, triumph, despair, and salvation. The saving message is that God will never let us go, even in the valley of death. These are the thoughts that may guide you as you reflect on ways to share your faith with your children during difficult times. The following are tools to help you in this process:

In the event of divorce:

- Reassure your children that it's not their fault.
- Explain the reason for the divorce at least every six months and answer your children's questions.

- Children need to know they're as loved as earlier.
- Don't force your children to take sides by making disparaging remarks about the former spouse to them or within earshot.
- Don't confide in your children (they are children, not spouses).
- Don't make them feel guilty if they enjoy being with your former spouse and relatives, and don't use your children as a means of getting even.
- Establish new or reinforce old family rituals and work toward reshaping your family identity.

In the event of death:

No two children are alike. Each will experience grief in his or her way. Kubler-Ross popularized the five stages of grief in her book *On Death and Dying*—denial, anger, bargaining, depression, and acceptance. But please remember, the defined stages are there to help us understand our grief and the grief of our children. They're not peg holes into which one may be fitted. You do better to try and identify and help in the stage your child is in rather than trying to funnel her through the stages in a systematic order.

Grief is what the child feels inside, but mourning is the action exhibited, which may include crying, hostility, aggression, withdrawal, or indifference. Be aware that each child mourns differently, and be available to comfort and reassure rather than focus on his or her behavior.

Mourning and grief are a process, not an event. We don't know how long a child grieves. Acceptance has occurred when he or she resumes activities, is happy, and rarely mentions the loss. Be sensitive to the type of comfort, support, and nurture you need to provide for each age-group.

Concealing your grief may make a child feel that the sadness and depression in the home are his or her fault.

Express your feelings. The children can then understand your sadness and be free to express their wide range of feelings and questions. As you talk together, remember that children are factual, so give clear, accurate descriptions. Statements like "good people go to heaven," or "death is like sleeping" can conjure up all kinds of fears and worries in your child's mind. Continue to share your faith by assuring them of God's love and presence in these critical times. Recite Psalm 23 and the Lord's Prayer together often. Hold each other as you do so. Your arms, hugging your child, represent the loving arms of the Almighty, who is seen by the young child through you, your actions, and your faith.

How can I encourage faith and spirituality during my child's crisis?

Crisis and the ensuing mourning and grief are a part of your faith journey with your child. You cannot insulate or protect your child from life's harsh realities. You can, however, help your child through these times not only by using the suggestions made but also by living and sharing your faith. Help provide divine comfort to your child. The young child feels comforted when you hold her. Words from a children's hymn or psalm and the sound of your voice may be assuring. The young focus on immediate need, and thus this process will have to be repeated often. Older children will have a greater need to talk things out and receive reassurance. Be prepared for potential crisis with older children by making booklets containing Bible verses that comfort and encourage. Read them together and be open to further questions, sharing of memories, and expressions of grief.

Our child's faith may move far beyond what we share or what we think he or she can grasp. We can't ignore our children's innate God-given spiritual center. Small ones may not be able to put the name God to their experience, but older ones may gain insights, wisdom, and a sense of God-presence surprising to us. An elderly woman said, "My mother died when I was in second grade, and a few years later, my father lay dying. The evening of his death, my brother and I saw a gentle, ethereal face at the window with cloudlike hair. It looked in, smiled softly, was gone, and then came back several times. I was sure God sent mother or an angel to comfort us. I felt warm inside." A young child's simple faith may console us when we least expect it. "Don't cry, Daddy," a four-year-old said as she stroked her father's cheek. "Mommy is happy. She's with Jesus and she's dancing."

Travel tips

The storm is over, but the memory of that frightening hour will stay with you for some time. That's what storms do. As you continue your walk, let me again give you some thoughts to reflect on as you move forward.

1. Crisis affects all family members. Attention is diverted from routine family life to the one in crisis. Be aware of this.

2. During a major crisis, you may be immersed in your own pain and find it difficult to function. Don't neglect your children, even when it appears they are not as affected. They may not be able to express their feelings.

3. The sense of loss and powerlessness brought on by crisis are expressed in many ways. Grief is a process. Talk out feelings.

4. When crisis has occurred and the acute grief has become prolonged, the child or adult may feel hesitant about re-engaging in life or taking risks. Plan events to help your family step back into life.

For review and response

Recap

1. There is much in life over which we have no control.

2. We wish and pray that our children could be protected from suffering and pain. Yet we have to recognize that they are as vulnerable as we in the face of the sudden, unexpected tempests that burst into their unsuspecting lives.

3. We must never underestimate the element of crisis in our child's life. Children have little experience on which to build, so minor events appear catastrophic and final to them.

4. Family crisis may be experienced differently by the young, because of their concrete, self-centered thinking.

5. The most critical crises a child faces is that of divorce or parent or sibling death.

6. Crisis and the ensuing mourning and grief are a part of your faith journey with your child. You can help your child through these times by living and sharing your faith. Help provide divine comfort to your child.

What then shall we do?

1. Don't wait until a crisis occurs before you communicate the resilience of the human spirit and the belief that God can help them face any hardships or crises that come their way. Find and tell stories in the Bible and in past or contemporary church history that can strengthen the courage of your children to face life against the odds. Read and discuss books like *Sara's Trek* by Florence Schloneger (Faith & Life Press, 1981).

2. Learn to ask for and receive help during critical times. This may come through extended family, support groups, talking with your pastor, or family counseling. As the

feelings of loss pass the critical stage, engage yourself and your child in decisions that restore hope and meaning. Tell the post-resurrection stories to your children—the grief and despondency followed by hope (Luke 24 and John 20—21).

3. Don't submerge your own feelings. Talking about the loss, reviewing memories, crying together, holding, and hugging are a part of healing and makes your child feel a participant in your life. But make wise judgments about how openly and often to display your grief. Too much, too long may frighten young children. Don't expect your children to be your comforters. Find another adult or extended family member with whom to share your grief.

4. As part of healing, make sure everyone takes care of him or herself. Each one may need more rest, may do something special for him or herself, and engage in some close family times. Recreation (re-creating) also encourages well-being. Praying together gives a sense of cohesion and partnership.

For family

Family time

1. *Bible crisis activities.* Reinforce Bible stories with related activities. Here are ideas for crisis times. Think of others.

Luke 15:3-7: The lost and hurt lamb is found by a caring shepherd. Relate to a crisis, such as illness, a time of loneliness, or moving. Reassure children of your love and God's love. Draw lamb shapes on heavy paper and cut them out, one for each family member. Glue cotton balls onto the lambs. Use buttons for eyes.

John 18:15-18, 25-27: Peter got scared and denied his friend. Relate to the crisis of denial or betrayal by one's best friend. How can the friendship be restored? (See 21:15-17.) Cut people from paper and tape them together at the hands to make a circle of friendship. Write names on the figures.

John 19:25-27: Jesus' mother is near him during his suffering. Relate this to your family crisis: Look at photos. Ask members to share by finishing "I feel sad because ..." or, "I miss _____ because. ..." Shared grief makes it bearable.

2. *Survival skills.* Children should learn age-appropriate skills that help them avert or survive a crisis: (a) household skills, such as laundry, cleaning, cooking; (b) emergency skills, such as dialing the police or fire station, what to do when accosted by a stranger, and what to do or not do when home alone. Write instructions on posters (use pictures for younger ones). Create hypothetical situations and act them out; (c) relational skills, such as how to respond when another child tries to pick a fight or threatens you. Discuss options.

3. *Write, call, pray.* Share your faith by involving your children in ministry to others. Write a note to a sick friend. Call or visit an elderly shut-in. Make a sympathy card for a family in grief. Invite children and parent in the process of divorce to your home, or take over a casserole. Look for critical events in your newspaper. Pray for these persons.

4. *Storytellers.* Jesus was a master storyteller. Build family (or extended family) togetherness through fun with storytelling. During a crisis, this serves as a brief distraction. Sit in a circle. One person starts a story (true, read, or made up). When he or she stops, the next person continues the story. Keep going until a teller announces, "The End."

5. Make a mosaic. Crush washed, colored eggshells, putting each color into a separate container. On heavy paper design a picture to give to a family member or friend going through crisis. Leave two inches/five centimeters free at the bottom. Spread glue on the drawing and lay down eggshells to create a mosaic. Find and agree on an encouraging Bible verse to print in the open space.

Celebrate the family

Celebrate February 14. Attributed by some to an early church bishop, St. Valentine's Day provides extra opportunities for showing love. Have children cut out red paper hearts and glue them onto paper doilies. Write the children's names onto slips, mix, and have each draw a name. On their heart, have them write "I love you because _____." When finished, have children give their card to the one whose name they drew. Parent(s) make a large heart with a love message for each child on it. Read 1 John 4:7. For a snack, make popcorn and mix in heart-shaped candy.

An idea for a family night activity

Family shapes. About 50 percent of North American children live in nuclear families. Others are in single-parent, blended (stepparent), and foster-parent families. Some children are raised by grandparents or other relatives. Invite families with other shapes than your own for an evening of popcorn and videos or games. If you become friends, share your time more often.

For study

Search the Scriptures

"Who shall separate us from the love of Christ? Shall trouble or hardship or persecution or famine or nakedness or danger or sword? ... No, in all these things we are more than conquerors through him who loved us" (Romans 8:35, 37).

What crises could cause a person to give up on God? (Romans 8:35, 38-39).

What is the difference between never being separated from the love of God and being protected from all danger and crisis?

Discuss the questions

1. Is a crisis defined by the event or by how that person experiences the event? Why do some experience crisis differently than others?

2. In what ways and why are crises in the lives of children different from those of adults?

Engage in group response

1. Discuss ways in which group members could support each other during times of crisis. If appropriate, make a written covenant with each other.

2. React to the following: "It's easy to believe in God when things are going well, but does God really look after us? Perhaps we have to look after ourselves in good times and bad."

3. Death is the final crisis over which we have no control. How would you want to be remembered? Write your epitaph and share with your group.

Chapter 10

Through a Sun-Speckled Woods

Discipling Children

....

Dark shadows

Only distant rumblings remind you of the storm as you and your children stumble out of the dark shack into a world of liquid sunshine. Birds are singing and raindrops drip lazily from leafy, green bushes bent low with the weight of the afternoon downpour. The world is serene and beautiful. Mud clogs your shoes as you head for the path, but there's no turning back now. You are well past the halfway mark and will soon reach the edge of the woods. Oh, stop for a moment and look up at the loveliness in the east. A bright rainbow etches beauty and hope against the dark receding clouds.

You walk carefully in the sunlight and even more carefully as you enter the dark woods. The overgrowth is heavy and tangled here. It's almost impossible to see where one is walking. Your oldest removed his shoes because of the mud, but cries out in pain as he steps on a hard rock. You stop to console him and guide him along the outer edge of the path.

Finally, you and your children reach an opening, and the sunlight filters through the tall trees. You look around, relieved, and then notice ... a child is missing. Your heart beats fearfully. You slip and slide in the mud, hurrying back, calling her name. A cry from the dark shadows below identifies her whereabouts. You kneel and coax her to climb back up. Soon the mud-covered child emerges, frightened, but unharmed. Reaching out, you half pull her up, soothe, and comfort her. You suggest she stay near you from now on. All move back to the sunlit opening. A moment's rest and you're walking toward the sun-speckled woods ahead, not knowing how many shadow places or sunny spots you'll encounter before reaching the meadows beyond.

This muddy experience is not unlike the daily routines of life with our children. We would like the paths to be smooth, dry, and clutter free, but it isn't always that way. Days are never all sunny. They are a series of sun and shadow, good and trying times, much like your moments of trouble in the sun-speckled woods.

One of the difficult areas we parents have to deal with is that of disciplining our children. Sunday school teachers often say, "I want to teach the little ones because they aren't a discipline problem." Note that the focus is on discipline as a problem. Is discipline a negative word for you? Most parents don't enjoy disciplining their children because they're not sure what is meant by the word "discipline." They're not sure what should be happening in the process nor very clear about the intended outcome. Is it only to stop certain behaviors? which ones? When do you or don't you discipline? What is effective discipline?

Repeatedly, things become muddy and we're not sure how to handle situations when our children get into trouble, disobey, or defy us. Sometimes we feel as though we're groping around in the shadows, wondering what we should or should not do. We tend to separate the discipline, the mud, and dark shadows from the rest of the sun-filled journey rather than seeing it as one whole. These are normal concerns and questions, all rooted in deeper questions about the nature and purpose of discipline.

What is the difference between violence and punishment?

Violence is not punitive; it is the physical venting of rage and frustration on one who is weak and helpless. Family violence is increasing at an alarming rate. More than 1 million cases of child abuse and neglect were reported last year in the United States, and of these, twelve hundred children died. Violence is merciless beating or torture. In our city, during this year alone, a father hit a four-month-old, breaking her leg and causing a concussion; a mother broke the arm of a four-month-old; foster parents beat a four-year-old to death. Violence is the merciless rape of a small child by a parent or the torture of the helpless. I've been told of small children scorched in frying pans or tortured with lit cigarette butts. Need I say more? Violence has nothing to do with punishment or discipline.

Punishment, on the other hand, is for some people a form of discipline. It is rooted in the patriarchal view of child raising that says "Spare the rod and spoil the child." When we think of punishment, it usually refers to spanking the child. Some parents believe it serves a purpose. A woman said, "When the little one throws a tantrum, I give him a few whops on the seat, he cries, relaxes, and becomes good-humored again." Another says, "Children have to know who is in charge."

The problem is that spanking doesn't teach or guide. It focuses on the moral level of development that dominates our society, "If you do wrong and get caught, you get punished." Our prisons are full of adults and youth being punished but not rehabilitated. Punishment by spanking puts all power and control in the hands of the parents. Parents decide what is right and wrong, and the children need to toe the line accordingly. If all misbehavior or mistakes are treated the same way, how is the child to learn when his actions have really been wrong or when they were due to a mistake? An older man said to me, "I loved my father, but he spanked us so hard for any small provocation, it made me afraid of him." Some parents rely on that fear to keep their children in line.

Spanking is the easiest way to effect punishment because the parent does not have to think about guidance, how to instruct the child toward mature, responsible behavior, or how to help that child take full responsibility for her behavior. The parent also holds all responsibility for decisions about appropriate physical punishment. Are rulers, switches, belts, or only hands appropriate? What wrongdoings lead to whipping? How much is enough for a particular act?

Discipline that uses spanking may for the parent appear momentarily successful if behavior is changed, but is it an effective means of guiding one's child? In chapter 8 we noted that primarily SJ children benefit from this form of discipline. The SPs don't change and the NF and NT children feel demeaned by this treatment. A woman said, "I tried walking across the yard with my eyes closed, stumbled over a farm implement, hurt myself, and got spanked. It seemed so unfair!" An elderly man said, "Father beat us for anything." You could still hear the sad pain in his voice.

I cannot forbid you to spank, but I want you to think seriously about these questions: Do we advocate violent behavior when we hit our children? Does our size and strength permit us to behave in ways that our children are not allowed to emulate? Would we spank our children if they were as tall as we are? Do we spank because that's how we maintain our authority in the family? Would we want our heavenly Parent to treat *us* this way?

When does punishment become abuse?

There are forms of punishment other than spanking. But in all punishment, the goal remains the same—that of getting the child to change her behavior and act as we would have her do. It has little to do with the child's personal volition, guidance towards helping that child make better decisions next time, or experiencing consequences directly related to the offense. One of the difficulties that punishing parents face is discerning the fine line between punishment and abuse. Punishment becomes abuse when it is the venting of parental rage or it is out of proportion to the infraction. Grounding a child for two weeks for not making her bed is abuse. When a child comes home late from school and is whipped with a belt, that is abuse. When a child breaks a dish and is struck across the face, that is abuse.

Another form of physical abuse is experienced through inconsistent punishment. A child lives in fear when the rules aren't clear and he is never sure which behaviors will merit a whipping. Another form of physical violence is sexual abuse, a problem increasingly common (or, at least increasingly known about) even in Christian homes. I read a story of a woman whose father, a leading deacon in their church, repeatedly raped her from age two. Parental behavior like this or any form of sexual abuse including inappropriate touch and fondling must never be tolerated.

Emotional and verbal abuse are also forms of punishment used to control the child. A parent who tyrannizes the family uses fear to control. Fear is used in many ways through threats or freezing out the child with unspoken disapproval. A woman said, "I was afraid of my father because he wouldn't talk to me or ever show approval." Fear can also be used as a physical weapon. A mother told me, "When Bud was three years old, my mother and I would put him in a roaster if he didn't behave, shove him in the oven, and threaten to turn on the gas." She laughed as she described his frightened screams.

Other forms of abuse are the use of cruel teasing or sarcasm. The child is violated and demeaned by such a parent into cringing obedience. Verbally venting parental rage on a cowering young one is another form of abuse. There are many other forms of abuse, but reviewing even a brief list raises our awareness and enlightens our conscience.

Are punishment and permissiveness related to each other?

We tend to treat our children the way we were treated. Or we bend the other direction and treat them just the opposite of how we experienced discipline. Parents who grew up in strict, forbidding homes are often too permissive. Because they had to do what they were told without thinking or being part of the process, they have not developed tools for guiding a child. Not wanting to treat their children the way they were treated, they allow a permissive home atmosphere where limits are not set, and the child takes over. These parents need to develop tools for guiding the child.

Many parents are afraid of rejection. They are so caught up with wanting their children to love them that they allow them free rein. Other parents are extremely permissive because they have no desire or are too exhausted to invest the energy, time, and warmth it takes to parent. Some parents vacillate between permissiveness and punishment because they themselves are struggling with issues of powerlessness and control rooted in their own strict upbringing. If parents are too lax, it may be because they find it hard to think of alternate ways to guide the child into a life of good decisions, moral values, and a love for God.

Punishment and permissiveness are related only in terms of one being a reaction against the other. The difficulty is that children may experience both of these parental behaviors as loveless. If the punitive outweighs love and warmth in the home, this growing child experiences that environment as loveless. If permissiveness reigns, this child takes charge and often becomes a little tyrant who creates a chaotic family environment. Children don't have the skills and training for taking control and may find too much freedom quite frightening. They may ask, "If Mom or Dad allow me to do anything I want, do they even care what I do or don't do? Do they love me enough to set limits?"

Parents can be empowered to look at options other than punishment or permissiveness. The goal of discipline is to raise your children to respect and live by Jesus' Great Commandment (Matthew 22:37-40).

What is the difference between discipline and discipling?

We've defined punishment, permissiveness, and abuse, but have only alluded to discipline. Webster's definition of discipline refers to both *punishment* and *teaching*. Because of this definition, I suggest we change the word *discipline* to *discipling*. What is the difference between the two? The difference is one of semantics, but as noted above, discipline has become closely associated with punishment in our society. Therefore, it is hard to perceive it as something other than that.

The word discipling is rooted in the word disciple and challenges parents to think in a fresh way about nurturing their children toward a personal faith and a mature lifestyle. We get our best definitions by looking at Jesus and his disciples. Even though these followers were adults, Jesus' methods embody ways to nurture and guide, which can be transcribed to the discipling of our children. Look at the following:

Jesus called the Twelve and spent much time teaching them. He was clear about his values and faith priorities and communicated them openly. He answered the disciples' questions. Much of their learning occurred through direct participation in his activities, observing how his mission took shape, and feedback after a miracle, healing, or instruction. As the Twelve matured, Jesus sent them out in twos to test their wings and report back. He allowed them to learn through their mistakes and gave them further instruction about how to do things differently next time. When they argued, Jesus pointed them to their real purpose in life. He taught them to pray, and they were with him when he prayed for them. Jesus asked them to stay with him in Gethsemane during his most difficult time, even though he knew their limitations. This was one more step in guiding them toward further growth. They were part of his most intimate circle. Even when they regressed through denial and running away, Jesus, at the end of his three years with them, entrusted them with a final message and mission to the whole world. Jesus allowed the disciples to learn and grow by teaching them to think, guiding them in decision making, and allowing them to experience the natural consequences of their chosen behaviors.

Let's relate this directly to our children. We don't own them. Through birth, adoption, or foster care, we called them into our families. Through instruction, guidance, modeling, and witness, we lead them toward faith and greater maturity. Children have little life experience. In our eyes they do some misguided things at times, but they are not bad or sinful.

Their lack of experience is the essential difference between children and adults. Therefore, they need more guidance and direction as they learn right from wrong.

Our discipling must be acted out in the context of the child's age and stage of development. At the same time, we must see our children as sacred beings whom we must treat with the same respect we give any adult. We need to help our children learn from their mistakes, disobedience, and wrong behavior by using natural or logical consequences. At the same time, we need to assure them that making a bad choice or misbehaving does not make them a bad person. By the use of guidance and natural consequences, we direct our children toward maturity by positive rather than negative means. Discipling has many implications for how our children perceive God and how they will later understand their growth toward a mature spirituality.

How can natural consequences for all ages be effected in discipling?

Natural consequences suggest a way of learning and discipling we experience throughout life. If you don't put oil in the car, you ruin it. If you're constantly late for work, you lose your job, and so on. Children are not wise or mature enough to learn without guidance, so parents need to teach them by creating appropriate consequences. Consequences are directly related to your child's behavior and provide an opportunity for her to learn from the experience. Here are several guidelines to keep in mind:

1. Take the age of your child into consideration. A two-year-old who doesn't know right from wrong can be picked up and removed with a firm "no," whereas an older child may choose between consequences or even come up with his own (they're often harder on themselves than parents are).

2. Listen to your child; look at the situation from his perspective and level of development. Hear his side of the story before deciding what natural consequences to use in teaching optional ways of behaving.

3. If the child has already learned through the experience (for example, cut herself when she was forbidden to use the sharp knife), there is usually no need to impose further consequences.

4. Determine what you believe to be right or wrong, and let your children know. Don't say no to everything, but be consistent in your selections. Begin with those that endanger the child. As children get older and you hear their side, you may need to be more flexible and negotiable.

5. Realize that the process changes with the years. A two-year-old hitting a child can merely be picked up and relocated. But ten-year-old siblings fighting may need to spend an hour in their room thinking, writing about how they can change the situation, and then coming to an agreement with each other.

Natural consequences to behaviors make sense and allow parents to treat their children with respect. They focus on the situation rather than the feelings so that children can learn from their behavior. Their intent is to disciple the child and to help him learn from the experience. With Jesus as your model, you will be able to share faith with your children through both shadows and sunshine.

Travel tips

As the path dries, walking becomes easier and the children have resumed their playful mood. Here are several more things to reflect on as you guide your children toward faith and maturity.

1. When your child does something wrong, take a deep

breath and relax. You can't help your child learn from an experience if you explode.

2. At times you may allow your children to learn from their mistakes without adding further consequences. For example, if you gave your school-aged child money for a friend's birthday gift and she spends it on candy, she'll have to face her friend at the party without a gift or find an ingenious way to make one. Don't bail her out.

3. Try to understand the reasons your child misbehaves. Some children misbehave to get attention. If parents are emotionally absent or too busy to give their time, the child may feel unloved and try to get attention through negative means. Some children misbehave because they are feeling bad about themselves, or because they are afraid and feel they need to protect themselves.

4. Be aware of the child's stages of disequilibrium, when new growth impels them toward testing the boundaries. As they grow older, they develop some of their own ideas. Parents need to review the rules without backing away from basic moral precepts which are important to the household.

5. Part of the discipling process is to give your child an increasing amount of responsibility for certain behaviors. As she grows older, and you treat her with respect and are clear about your expectations, your child will be more likely to act in appropriate ways. If she regresses in some areas, you may have to review that behavior with her and/or impose consequences.

For review and response

Recap

1. One of the difficult areas we parents have to deal with is that of disciplining our children. Sometimes we feel we're groping around in the shadows, wondering what we

should or should not do.

2. Violence is not punitive; it is the physical venting of rage and frustration on the weak and helpless.

3. Spanking is the easiest way to effect punishment because the parent doesn't have to think about guidance, how to instruct the child toward mature, responsible behavior, or how to help that child take full responsibility for his behavior.

4. Punishment becomes abuse when it is the venting of parental rage or if it is out of proportion to the infraction.

5. We tend to treat our children the way we were treated. Or we bend the other direction and treat them just the opposite of how we experienced discipline.

6. The word *disciple* is rooted in the word discipline. Discipling challenges parents to think in fresh ways about nurturing their child toward personal faith and a mature lifestyle.

7. Natural consequences suggest a way of learning and discipling that we experience through life. Children are not wise or mature enough to learn without guidance, so parents need to teach them by creating appropriate consequences.

What then shall we do?

Think about the significance of forgiveness and hope as you disciple your child.

1. The essence of family life is relationships. Misbehaviors or bad choices can unbalance the equilibrium. Encourage your child when her behavior begins to improve so that she can live in hope. Hope creates the stamina and vision that stimulates further change.

2. A child's bad judgment or misbehavior may be an expression of a new stage of growth. Talk with your child about the behaviors and decide whether it's time to back off on some issues. If you have wronged your child by imposing unjust consequences, ask for forgiveness.

3. If you are angry and disappointed with your child, talk about those feelings and then forgive. No child deserves ongoing anger and the distrust of parents. Keep before you the example of Peter. Despite his denial, Jesus forgave him, reestablished the relationship, and entrusted Peter with new responsibilities.

For family

Family time

1. *Talking feelings.* When we share feelings, we strengthen family relationships and learn skills needed to talk out difficult discipling issues. Have family members finish the following, then share and discuss:

I feel angry when _____. I feel happy when _____.
I feel warm inside when _____. I feel hurt when _____.
I feel disappointed when _____. I feel afraid when _____.

2. *Taking your picture.* Give each family member a tube from toilet tissue, paper, pencil, and crayons. Write names on paper slips, mix, and have each one draw a name. You are photographers, taking a picture of the one whose name you drew. Aim the roll at the person, look through it, focus on a part of that person, and draw a picture. Emphasize the part you think is special. For example, if friendly, draw in a big smile; if curious, draw big eyes; or if loving, draw a big heart. Share. Discuss: "What makes our family special?"

3. *Shape collage.* In advance, cut out many shapes, such as triangles, squares, half circles, etc., using black and white paper. Tell a story about a significant family event, and ask each one to re-create the situation or the feelings about it by arranging the various shapes on the table. Ask each one to share his or her collage.

4. *Who done it?* Discuss what might have caused the

following remarks.

"My kitchen floor is covered with muddy footprints!"

"The cookie jar is empty already!"

"There are wet towels on the bathroom floor!"

"Dinner is getting cold. Where is _____ (a family member's name)?"

Add other remarks common to your family situation. Talk about how our behaviors affect others.

5. *Joy germs.* The gospel makes us joyful (Philippians 4:4a). Joy is catching. Everybody invents and cuts a number of Joy Germs from stiff paper and decorates them. Announce a day when each one tries to bring joy, happiness, or laughter to another and then gives that person a Joy Germ. At the end of the day, count up how many germs were spread in the family. Hold hands and thank God for joy in your family.

Celebrate the family

Celebrate Pentecost. Review the significance of the Holy Spirit as described in chapter 2 before you share the Pentecost story from Acts 2. Tell the story or read it from the simply told book *God Keeps His Promises* (Evangel Press, Faith & Life Press, and Herald Press, 1970, p. 165). Create a banner: Make flame patterns; have children draw around them on colored pieces of cloth and cut them out. Glue the flames above the heads of stick figures you have drawn on the banner. "The Holy Spirit Gives Power" may be printed below. Note that Jesus is alive, and God's Spirit has been sent to help and guide us. Celebrate Pentecost by hanging the banner and singing "Halleluja." Clap or accompany with a kitchen band, using spoons, glasses, pots, and pans.

Hallelujah

Words and Music by Anne N. Rupp

Hal - le - lu - jah, Hal -le - lu - jah, Hal - le - lu - jah, Hal - le - lu.

Hal - le - lu - jah, Hal -le - lu - jah, Hal - le - lu - jah, Hal - le - lu.

Hal - le - lu - jah!   Hal - le - lu!   Hal - le - lu - jah

An idea for a family night activity

Tree house or playhouse. Jesus often withdrew to a quiet place when tired. Spend several Family Nights building a tree house or playhouse with your children. Suggest they use it as a place of their own to play, read, or listen to music.

For study

Search the Scriptures

"I will instruct you and teach you in the way you should go; I will counsel you and watch over you" (Psalm 32:8).

Select the four verbs from this passage. How are they related to discipling?

The psalmist goes on to say that when he confessed his wrongdoing, he experienced forgiveness, not punishment. How is this like or unlike your childhood experience?

Discuss the questions

1. How would you define the difference between effective and successful discipline?

2. Why is the process of discipling your children difficult? How does it change your way of thinking about discipline?

Engage in group response

1. On newsprint, draw five columns and make a list of adjectives that describe each of the following practices in child rearing: violence, abuse, punishment, discipline, and discipling. Discuss the fine distinctions between each.

2. On sheets of paper, have each person doodle a sketch representing his or her most frequently used form of discipline. Discuss: "My approach does or does not meet the criterion for discipling." "My approach does or does not meet my needs more than the child's."

3. What does discipling have to do with "shalom," the biblical word for peace? Identify examples in the Bible that depict poor or wise parenting. What does it mean to you when we say, "Treat your children the way God treats us." What does that say about discipling? Share and discuss.

Chapter 11

In the Shadow of the Mighty Oak

How Children Learn about Responsibility and Freedom

From acorns to oaks

After hiking through mud, climbing over rocks to avoid puddles on the path, and shading eyes against the intense rays of the after-storm sun, it's a relief to reach the cool darkness under this sturdy, old oak. You stand under the spreading, gnarled branches and feel minuscule. As you gaze up into the branches, it is not only your diminished height but also a sense of your finiteness that overwhelms you. This grizzled, time-worn oak under which you stand was here long before you existed and will probably be here to see your children, grandchildren, and great-grandchildren stroll through the woods on summer days. I felt this way in Mt.

Rainier National Park last summer when we hiked to the
Grove of the Patriarchs, gargantuan spruce trees on an island
untouched by forest fire for centuries. How dwarfed my six-
foot height seemed beside these giants; how brief my lifespan
and insignificant my problems in the light of so much age.

We sometimes forget that a child, diminutive in size
compared to our height, may feel this way in our presence.
We represent shade and shelter for this young one. But our
height, knowledge, and experience can also be intimidating.
If we look at the nurture and faith growth of our child only
from our perspective, we forget that vintaged oaks come from
acorns. We can't just take over for our children or protect
them from the harsh realities of life. The faith we share with
them must model more than helplessness and total dependence on God. It must demonstrate Christ's call to responsible
discipleship within the boundaries of Christian freedom. To
do this adequately, we must deal with issues of power and
control in the family, because these factors determine how
responsibility and freedom intertwine in the gristmill of our
family's daily life.

When we look at the confusing messages emerging
from our society, the issues we are discussing in this chapter
become increasingly pertinent. Many seek religious experience to help them cope or make them feel good without the
demands of discipleship. Charlatans urge people to sue for
any reason. Have you ever tried to issue a complaint, and
found yourself shuffled from one staff person to another
because no one accepts responsibility? How often have you
picked up cans and paper from your front lawn because people choose not to use the wastebasket in their cars? Everyone
is looking out for #1, with a limited sense of respect or
responsibility. One could go on and on. In contrast, our faith
must communicate a higher plane of living, a lifestyle in

which the joy and daring of Christian freedom is never separated from responsibility. This raises many questions.

What is the difference between control and power?

An older man once said to me, "Years ago a psychologist said that the first thing you have to do in child rearing is
break the child's will!" This patriarchal mentality aims to control the child as an object which must be bent or shaped. Yet
some parents who would loudly protest against such thinking
find subtle (or not so subtle) ways to control their children.

There are many forms of control: continually saying no
to a young child; excessive or uncalled for punishment; constantly telling a child what to do without considering the
child's needs or point of view; sarcasm, put-downs, and other
ways of demeaning the child. Lack of respect for the child,
intimidation, hitting across the face, or walking into an older
child's room without permission all convey the message "I
own you." Another form of control is exhibited by well-meaning parents who try to protect their child from any difficulty.
Parents also control when they assume their youngster isn't
capable of exercising initiative or tackling new tasks. Both
approaches focus on the immaturity, not the potential, of the
child. These children may become insecure, fearful, and
dependent. They will have difficulty acting responsibly unless
they are eventually able to break away from the control.

In some homes, the children control the parents. They
have learned through tantrums, sulking, demands, and manipulation how to sabotage family relationships and get their
way. Vulnerable parents, often isolated from family support,
fear they will lose the child's love. So they cater to the whims
and fancies of the child. Control—whether by parent or child—
creates unhealthy relationships. Is there another way?

We need to realize that healthy spiritual development occurs when faith is shared in an environment where all are valued. The word "power" is akin to "empower." To grow and develop, children need to be given a sense of power appropriate for their age.

Power is given in the early years by expressed encouragement when the child tries something new. It is shared by allowing decisions that are appropriate for a child's age (see chapter 6). Power is not to be abdicated by the parent, nor are the parents to engage in permissiveness (the opposite of control) that says "Do whatever you want!" It is given when we progressively entrust a child with certain behaviors, choices, and responsibilities and let him know we trust him to carry through. Power is given when we respect the child's personality, never ridicule or laugh at his actions, give consideration to his ideas, and commend him for positive behavior or action he initiates.

Power is not like a fence you build around yourself, fearing the child will undermine your authority if you allow her to exert individuality. It is more like a door leading into a house with many rooms. You invite your child in to care for a room and add other rooms as she matures and is able to handle power appropriately. When we empower our children, we treat them the way God treats us. God is not a mighty oak who keeps us dependent, but one who gives shade and shelter when we need it and then expects us to take on fuller responsibility for our lives. When we model empowered, responsible Christian lives for our children, we also give the faith message "This is what God is like!"

What does power have to do with freedom and responsibility?

In the early church, freedom in Christ was interpreted by some as a form of lawlessness: You could do anything you want to do and God in Jesus Christ would forgive you. An interpretation of freedom that allows you to do your own thing regardless of how your behavior and attitude affect others is not freedom. There is no freedom without responsibility. True freedom means being released from imposed restrictions. You are able to be innovative, test new ways of thinking and acting, but always within the limits of responsibility. For the Christian, freedom means living within and beyond the expectations of the Great Commandment (Matthew 22:37-39) while taking our motives and the effects of our behavior on others into consideration.

If you allow your five-year-old to cross the street, you are giving that child power and ensuing freedom to play with her friend without you going with her. But if, despite instruction and example, you find her darting across the road, looking to neither left nor right, she misuses that freedom. You may have to withhold some of that power until she proves she can handle it.

Power, freedom, and responsibility are integral parts of growing up physically, emotionally, and spiritually. Your children will constantly and irresponsibly test the fine lines of power and freedom. It takes much Spirit guidance to handle each situation wisely so that this can become a part of the child's faith development and a means of expressing your own faith to your child. Remember, you share your faith when you model a joyful, meaningful relationship with God in which you determine how to live a responsible, innovative life as a disciple of Jesus Christ. Keep this in mind in the options you face and the way you give your children options. Treating your children as God treats you is a good guideline to understanding freedom and responsibility.

Are there ways I can help my child become more responsible?

We want our children to grow into responsible Christians who take their discipleship seriously. That growing starts now. Helping your child determine options and guiding her through decisions are crucial steps towards independent thinking and responsible behavior.

How would you feel if God was constantly telling you what to do? That's how some parents try to train their children. Some parents are still *telling* their child what to do in the late teen years. Children can become tone deaf and no longer listen. Either they won't exert themselves responsibly because they only function when told what to do, or they rebel. At the other end of the spectrum are the parents who allow their children free rein because they're too busy to participate in child rearing, or they believe training implies restriction of the child's natural impulses. These children grow up with little affirmation, hugging, or a parent's personal involvement. They're unaware of how best to learn a new task or take full responsibility for behavior.

One way of helping your child choose responsible behavior is depicted by Paul Hersey and Kenneth H. Blanchard in *The Family Game* (Addison-Wesley Publishing Company, 1980). Think of these steps, rooted in Hersey/Blanchard's ideas, as a guide for you to use:

1. Identify an area of responsibility or behavior that needs to be affected. Make sure the child is capable of managing the task. Don't make the task too big or move too fast. That sets him up for failure. Maturity is a relative term. Your child may be mature in one area and immature in another.

Involve your child in determining what to learn or change. Often parents give children only menial tasks to do instead of skills to achieve. Don't say: "I'd like you to set the table every evening," because no standards are set. Rather, say: "This is how I'd like you to ...," and demonstrate to the child.

2. After "show and tell," your child does the task with your strong affirmation. If she appears unable, demonstrate again until she can do it. Children feel proud when they learn and accomplish a new task.

3. When your child can do the task with little support, he may introduce other ideas about how to do it well. Peek in occasionally while he is occupied and say things like "I'm proud of the way you set the table and I really like the candle you decided to put in the middle." This helps the child know he can initiate new ideas and be appreciated.

4. Once the task is learned and done without further involvement, the child takes on full responsibility. I'd suggest a Responsibility Celebration (the frequency would depend on the age of the children; the young need more immediate responses) where everyone shares new things learned. Respect everyone's accomplishments, be they ever so small. Say a prayer of thanks to God who gives abilities, ideas, and strength to perform a task. The family community is a Christian model for encouragement, support, and affirmation.

If regression occurs, move back one step. Too readily we make angry demands, criticize, or go back to demonstrating. Return to demonstration only if moving back one or two steps doesn't work. Once the task has been performed for some time, your child is ready to learn another new task.

Faith is more than a good feeling. It is a lifestyle committed to discipleship that doesn't turn back or waft to and fro when things are going wrong. Witnessing to this understanding by word and behavior is a way of sharing your faith with your child. Helping your child become increasingly responsible prepares her for life under the lordship of Jesus

Christ. Responsibility is not learned overnight. It is a process that takes patience, guidance, and tolerance.

How can children learn responsible stewardship, service, and mission?

To learn stewardship, service, and mission, the child must first of all understand these concepts. How you and your family perceive stewardship is best taught by modeling. Stewardship involves more than money. An effective Christian steward believes that all we have and are is a gift of God, and we are entrusted to care for that gift during our short life span. Responsible stewardship incorporates both Genesis 2:15 and Matthew 22:37-40. We are keepers (not users) of the earth, relationally tied to God and others, as well as caretakers of our body and soul. We best exemplify stewardship by our environmental concerns and lifestyle, our care for others (whether local or distant), and our ability to respect and care for ourselves.

Stewardship also includes how we use our time. Our Protestant work ethic encourages workaholism, but responsible stewardship sets aside freeing time for reflection, rest, and play. Recreation means to be re-created. Modern life leaves little room for this balance when play becomes work, when even children's sports become competitive, and being busy is valued. Assess how you and your children regard time. How do you encourage a balance that respects the well-being of child and adult? How do you uphold and value time for relationships, family building, and sharing with others? Your conclusions are another way of sharing your faith with your children.

A final aspect of responsible stewardship concerns teaching children how to manage money at an early age. Start an allowance by age five or six with which they're responsible to buy one designated item and the rest is for their own discretionary spending. Increase allowance and responsibilities for it annually. They will spend foolishly at times, but living with the consequences is part of learning. Don't rescue them when they overspend. Don't bank their allowance for college. (If you do, you still control the money.) Encourage saving by matching funds for some major items they want to buy. Tithing must be volitional, but explained, taught, encouraged, and modeled. If you keep a world bank on your table and at weekly allowance time demonstrate benevolent giving, children will follow suit. Identify a project and later visit the site. Working together to write to the recipients or buying the items to be donated can be an incentive to sharing.

Children learn about responsible service and mission by what they perceive and experience. Mission and service are not something "out there"—it's you and your children being involved in various ways. Faith is not only shared in the family or with our children. Faith compels us to move beyond the boundaries of our home to the world outside. Begin with an open-door policy where all are welcome, where you deliberately become acquainted with those different from yourself and make them feel at home. Christian freedom moves us beyond self to caring for more than our own. It makes our children aware of the vast opportunities for service by the way we relate to others. Discrimination has no room in our Christian vocabulary and behavior. Share your faith with your children by witnessing to the fact that in Christ, we are all brothers and sisters.

Travel tips

The shadow of the mighty oak can represent overprotection and intimidation, or it can symbolize the security and dependability children need from their parents as they mature and grow in faith and life. Children gradually earn more power and take on more responsibility as they are allowed to practice appropriate freedom. By doing their own tasks and seeking alternatives, they discover ways of expressing themselves and begin to own their decisions. They become more capable of accepting responsibility for their behaviors, relationships, and concerns. As you leave this cool, refreshing spot, think further what the oak signifies for you and consider some additional tips for this last leg of your journey.

1. Children can learn that expressed faith is broader than their own immediate concerns. Talk about this and draw "before and after" pictures to give a vision for how we are or can be keepers of God's world. Better yet, pick up litter, write letters of concern about hazardous waste, plant a tree, or actively respect the natural beauty of nature in parks and campgrounds.

2. There are many ways to commit your family to service. Include your children in church clubs which emphasize service. Affirm Sunday school teachers who involve children in acts of service. Engage your family in local service projects, collections of Christmas gifts for the needy, and donations of food for the hungry. Assist a neighbor.

Create family role plays to help your children feel the indignity of those trapped in a cycle of poverty. Can they understand how demeaned the needy feel as recipients of someone's useless leftovers? Service in the name of Christ must be done as to a brother or sister, not from a sense of superiority. You model a responsible caring faith for your children by how you talk about and act toward those less fortunate.

3. Broadening our perspective and concern beyond our immediate personal or family situation leads to responsible living and decision making. Mission involvement is not only an act; it's a mentality, a way of life that is willing to give up something in order to share with others. Learn about mission. Invite

guest missionaries and speakers indigenous to other countries to your home. Write to missionary families and post their pictures on your refrigerator or bulletin board. Consider spending a family vacation volunteering time in evangelism work or a service project in a setting your denomination supports. Begin when the children are young so that mission engagement becomes a faith mentality affirmed and enjoyed by all.

For review and response

Recap

1. We can't just take over for our children or protect them from the harsh realities of life.

2. We need to realize that healthy spiritual development occurs when faith is shared in an environment where all are valued.

3. An interpretation of freedom that allows you to do your own thing, regardless of how your behavior and attitude affect others, is not freedom. There is no freedom without responsibility.

4. We want our children to grow into responsible Christians who take their discipleship seriously. That growing starts now.

5. To learn stewardship, service, and mission, the child must first of all understand these concepts. How you and your family perceive stewardship is best taught by modeling.

What then shall we do?

1. Assess whether you have open or closed communication in your family. In open communication, positive and negative feelings are encouraged, shared, and discussed. Expressions of acceptance (tempered with guidance) and affirmation empower your child.

2. Keep promises you make to your children. Children must experience you as trustworthy and dependable. By being so, you build their trust in God and model what it means to be Christ's follower.

3. Involvement is both an act and an attitude. Develop an open home policy where different cultures, races, religions, married, or single are welcome. Jesus was accused of eating with the wrong people. Who are the unacceptables or those looked down on in your community? What will you do?

For family

Family time

1. *Family rules.* In some families the rules are not clear or they change according to the whim of the parents. In both cases, children are less likely to accept responsibility because they feel confused about expectations. Rules need not be made only by parents. Cooperation is more likely if children can be involved in the rule-making process or feel that some negotiating can take place. Make a scroll from brown paper and staple dowels on each end. At the top print FAMILY RULES. Have everyone participate in listing rules (the do's and don'ts of living together), adding to them occasionally, or renegotiating those which don't seem fair. Review and adapt them several times a year, depending on new situations, circumstances, and ages of your children.

2. *Our family went to....* Become acquainted with the mission and relief needs of different countries or communities. Talk about one at a time throughout the year. Become acquainted with the geography, culture, history, and culture of the particular place. Use pictures and songs that best describe the place you are learning about. (Check your denominational headquarters or church for information.)

After you have talked about a place, sit in a circle and play a game. For example, the first one says, "Our family went to Egypt and took sunglasses." The next player must repeat what's gone before, adding his or her travel item related to the place they are visiting. Continue to go around the circle. When someone misses an item, they are out. The game is finished when only one player is left.

3. *Freedom cloth.* Buy a square of sailcloth and hem the edges. Provide crayons. Have each person draw a picture or symbol of what freedom means to him or her. When finished, lay the colored side down on waxed paper and iron to fix the color. Lay it on your table and ask members to share about their drawings. Talk about the difference between true freedom rooted in making responsible choices and lawlessness, which only thinks of getting what it wants and doesn't care about others. Whenever your family needs to call a council session around the table to discuss family issues, lay down the cloth as a reminder that the Christian family always wants to seek a balance between freedom and responsibility.

4. *Litter mission.* Some communities are organized to use volunteers to pick up roadside litter. If no organization exists, find a safe road where your family can pick up litter. You model service when you participate with your children in a project such as this. Wear brightly colored vests. Place the litter into plastic sacks and take them home for garbage pickup or other means of disposal. Model and share with your children the importance of being keepers of God's beautiful world. Children who labor to pick up litter are less likely to litter themselves. If your vehicles don't have wastepaper baskets, go as a family to shop for some. During family time, create a litany in which you describe your family experience. The response to each phrase could be "Thanks, God, for your beautiful world!"

5. *Haiku poem.* Involve your family in creative expressions about God. The Japanese haiku is a three-line unrhymed verse with five syllables in line one, seven in line two, and five in line three. Write one together or individually. Share. You could also use this form for personal expressions of faith, beginning with an affirmation such as "I believe God is" (line 1). This is an opportunity for you to share your faith and hear your children's faith ideas.

Celebrate the family

Celebrate Thanksgiving. A story is told of the pilgrims' first thanksgiving in what eventually became the United States. After a year of near starvation, they finally had food to eat and shared their thankfulness by eating together. To remind them of God's goodness, five kernels of corn were placed on each plate. Before the meal, each person picked up their kernels one by one and expressed thanks to God. For your Thanksgiving, dry ears of corn. Ask your children to put five kernels on each plate. At the table, tell the story of the pilgrims, and then follow their practice, each person expressing thankfulness for five things or experiences.

An idea for a family night activity

Giving glass. Together choose a financial mission project. Agree on a cash amount, or determine how many weeks you want to give towards this particular project. (You could also make this a special one-time event on Christmas Eve.) To make the Giving Glass, save eggshells; dye and crush them. Cover a glass with white glue and roll it in the broken shells. (Or use tiny pasta, such as acini de pepe. Mix with food coloring and dry before gluing.) Make Family Night allowance time. Each child decides how much (or if any) of his or her allowance will be put into the glass. Don't pressure or expect a fixed amount. Stewardship is learned from your example and stories you tell about the project. Upon completion, plan a brief family worship and together mail or deliver your gifts.

For study

Search the Scriptures

"Fathers [parents], do not exasperate your children; instead, bring them up in the training and instruction of the Lord" (Ephesians 6:4).

In what ways do parents exasperate their children? Why is this wrong?

What do the words "training" and "instruction" mean to you? What do they have to do with sharing your faith?

Discuss the questions

1. Think of a time your parents exasperated you. How did you feel?

2. What aspects of responsibility do you most want to share and model in your family?

Engage in group response

1. Comment on the following: "It is easier to control our children and make them feel powerless because empowerment takes energy and rational thought that takes into consideration the age, maturity level, and development of each child." Share ways in which you have given your children power.

2. How does your understanding of freedom and responsibility affect the way you share your faith with your children? Share and discuss.

3. Most of us have difficulty in following through on the steps for teaching responsibility because we don't identi-

fy our style. Draw four blocks horizontally and write in the four steps. Draw two lines underneath to make a triangle. Study the steps. Identify those most used by you and write them in the triangle. Share. What would you like to change?

Chapter 12

The Pond

Sharing Shalom with Children

....

Beside still waters

You reach a clearing and leave the trees behind. You have made a half-circle through the woods and are much closer to home than expected. To your left, someone is developing an arboretum. Green trees, lush grasses, shrubs, and flowers enhance the paths. In the middle, a large pond reflects the willows weeping along the edges. White wrought-iron benches beckon visitors to rest awhile. The water is quiet. Waves play gently along the shore. There is no indication of life beneath the surface, but we know it's there. The pond is stocked with fish. Frogs, toads, and snakes make their home in this insect paradise where they feed. You decide to take the shorter path through the arboretum rather than the longer one on the far side. Both lead toward home. Your children feed leftover crumbs to the ducks who seem to appear from nowhere, waddling toward you with their begging quacks. Enjoy the quiet moments as you take leave of your day in the woods.

There is a sense of shalom here, of well-being and quiet joy. The Hebrew word "shalom" means peace: a life lived in harmony with God, self, others, and one's environment. What does this say to you about the world in which you are raising and sharing faith with your children?

In an increasingly violent and abusive society, the environment is threatened by those who don't grasp the meaning of *keeping* the earth (stewardship of God-given resources). Murder, rape, beatings, robberies, kidnappings, forgeries, deceptions, deceit, and much more work against harmony. Forces like greed, self-centeredness, and self-interest destroy integrity, concern for others, and awareness of the long-range consequences of destructive behaviors. Nowhere is this more clearly expressed than in the sexual, physical, emotional abuse, and murders of young children, frequently by the parents. Christian parents cannot hide their heads in the sand. At the very moment they think they are immune to such behaviors, they may be seduced by their own sense of power or lack of conscience. Evidence shows that sexual, physical, and emotional abuse toward children and spouses occurs even in Christian homes. This fact raises many questions about shalom and our faith.

What does shalom have to do with faith?

The shalom described in Genesis 1–2, God's original intent for creation, was broken in Genesis 3 and replaced by intrigue, murder, falsehood, wars, and destruction. The prophets' calls to return to God went unheeded time and again. Only in Jesus Christ, through God's Essential Being, is shalom established once more. Christ's teachings in the Sermon on the Mount (Matthew 5–7) are the heartbeat of shalom. Shalom is possible; it lies at the center of every Christian's commitment, but can only be attained and lived out through the guidance and empowerment of God's Greater Spirit. It leaves no room for hypocrisy, judgment, slander, and all other forces that seek to destroy shalom. It is servanthood chosen, not subjugation imposed. It has only one Lord, and that is God. Shalom is not passive. It is a positive force that actively works toward God's intended purpose, the transformation of the world. Shalom cannot be separated from justice because oppression, discrimination, and abuse are anti-shalom. That's why shalom is difficult. Underneath the apparent calm are many forces which would disturb and destroy the harmony that God intends. Shalom stands at the center of our faith. We sometimes forget that the angelic proclamation in Luke 2:11-14 announced not only a Savior and Lord but also the intervention of God's glory into human history, bringing peace on earth and goodwill (shalom).

How does shalom fit into your relationship with God, self, others, and your environment? What kind of faith do you model for your children, based on your understanding of shalom? Think about these questions.

How can I share a God of shalom with children?

Shalom is not a concept; it is a relational reality central to one's profession of faith. Shalom is more than talk; it is a way of life. You cannot have a relationship with God through Jesus Christ unless the beams of the cross intersect: one beam stretching to God, one reaching out to others, both finding personal harmony at one's center, the point of intersection (Matthew 22:37-40).

Jesus' life and teaching exemplify shalom. The New Testament teaches that God is a caring, relational God who through Christ has restored harmony—a God who is love and a God of peace. When these beliefs are integrated with your faith, every aspect of your life—your thoughts, feelings, and actions—is positively affected. Paul calls it having the mind of Christ (1 Corinthians 2:16).

Putting an integrated faith into action requires beginning with certain premises. The first one is that all humans are created sacred. Regardless of class, gender, age, race, mental or physical capacity, culture or religion, each one is as important to God as we are. People who are poor or powerless are often treated with great indignity. They are looked down on in ways so subtle, even the protagonist is unaware of the messages being sent.

Be a sensitive parent. Try to identify with those who often feel powerless, and help your children do the same. Walk in the shoes of a child; a female; an elderly, single, or disabled person; or one with another skin color. Check your thoughts for bias and prejudice. What are some of the first words that come to mind? These test your level of acceptance. Are you ready to share a compassionate faith of acceptance with your children?

A New Testament faith as exemplified by Jesus—motivated by love, compassion, and shalom—leaves no room for prejudice or bias in any form. If you create an atmosphere of acceptance in your home, talk freely about what this has to do with your faith. Open your home to those deemed powerless. Provide toys and books that demonstrate concepts such as acceptance, understanding, and sharing across the lines of race, gender, age, and ability. Your child will soon assume that these values are essential ingredients of faith.

The second premise follows naturally: all are equal. No person is better than another. You share shalom with your children when you respect others, even those with whom you don't agree. During grade school and preadolescence, children tend to form small cliques. When a fifth grader moved to a small town and spent an afternoon with new friends, he came home and announced, "Now I know who's in and who's out." You cannot make your child play with or include another child, but you can model and share equality and acceptance at home. You can provide your children with resources to help them achieve empathy, understanding, and an open mind. Ephesians 2 notes that in Christ, who is our peace, all barriers have been broken down. Share that faith with your children.

What contemporary issues disrupt harmony?

Anti-shalom, or disharmony in society, provides subjects for many discussions you and your family may engage in. Here are several:

The greatest cause of disharmony in our global community is war and revolution. World leaders need to develop skills in negotiating and contracting that won't permit mass destruction of innocents by means of technological warfare. Until Vietnam, war was romanticized, and patriotism came before humanity. There is nothing romantic about war. War presents conflict for the Christian whose faith is rooted in shalom. I am a professing conscientious objector and could under no condition bear arms. My foreparents, the Anabaptists, gave their lives for this belief based on their understanding of Jesus' teachings (Matthew 5–7). Opposition to war, however, must never be passive. It must be rooted in shalom, which positively works toward peace in every aspect of life and society.

Take a hard look at the ruination taking place in the world between the haves and have nots, between countries with power using force to protect their vital interests, and between those who cannot resolve their turf, class, or boundary issues. This destruction affects every aspect of our faith life, because we are living in privileged nations of haves, whose smaller population consumes the greater amount of the world's goods. This is the world your children will one day inherit unless we take Christ's mandate to be peacemakers much more seriously. Share shalom with them now and be involved in the world's needs. Monitor their play. Does it mimic destructive aggression or the building of relationships? War and other violent toys only serve to propagate the myth of using negative means to achieve so-called positive ends.

Another great shalom concern is environmental. As population increases, technology impersonalizes, and people are no longer dependent on each other. As industry flourishes, the worth of the person is determined by productivity. And as capitalistic interests become the primary concern, the harmony of our ecosystem is disrupted by users rather than keepers of the earth. One of your faith concerns needs to be that of becoming informed. Then, with your family, act on your shalom convictions.

A final shalom concern is the influence of violence, sexism, and bias from television. Of equal concern are the ways commercials focus on immediate gratification, half-truths, and false promises. More money is spent on commercials aimed at children than on children's programming. Often advertised items don't meet up to the tantalizing expectations sold by the commercial. Advertising and programming both need to be looked at in the context of truth telling. By age six, I often heard our son say, "They're lying," when looking at a commercial. His opinion was reinforced when a much-advertised toy he asked for at Christmas broke two days later.

Our society has lost the meaning of truth telling. On TV and elsewhere in our society, we are repeatedly bombarded by lies, evasion, and manipulation. You need to be aware of what is happening so that you can discuss with children the meaning of broken promises, half-truths, and slander. Focus on the issues rather than on the individual, and help your child understand what truth telling is. It is not unusual for the values of Christians to contradict those of self-interested parties. You share your faith when you help your children see the difference.

What can we do about conflict and fighting?

Much conflict at home can be averted if everyone is treated with love and respect. Your children need to know they are loved, that you are trustworthy and genuine. This assurance builds self-esteem and a child who is confident, better able to share, and less self-centered. Hug your children frequently. As they get older, hold off on public displays, but remember to give hugs in private. Provide stuffed animals they can hug. By age four, a pet can provide a great sense of security and affection.

Conflict at home is often triggered by turf issues. Children need to know what space or possessions are theirs and be given the respect they deserve. When things are taken away or privacy intruded, the child may become defensive and less inclined to share. Conflict also occurs when children are competitive, feel left out, or don't get enough attention. When your children frequently fight and clamber for attention, assess the nature of emotional care and support you are giving.

There are many reasons for family conflict. Some have to do with power issues, and others are normal growing edges as the child exerts more independence. Rather than see anger and conflict as bad, teach and demonstrate how to negotiate so that each side can feel like winners. Let children know that anger is natural, but certain behaviors such as name calling, put-downs, yelling, and hitting are not appropriate. Guide them toward expressing feelings, such as "I feel left out when ..." or "I feel scared when ..." as you help them resolve differences or settle yours with them.

Never underestimate the power of laughter and humor in the family. It is God's gift to humans; it bonds a family, cuts down on tension, and helps resolve arguments. When I taught third graders, I often resolved tension by making up and singing silly ditties as instructions. Laughter followed, tension dissolved, and the class settled down.

Travel tips

The stillness of the pond mirrors only the surface, not the life below. Shalom is central to faith. Yet, when practically lived and shared, shalom is difficult to live by because it has so many aspects, each one with its particular positive and negative repercussions. For example, if all people of faith used only recycled products, some industries would suffer. If you teach your child not to fight, she may be beaten up by another. If you don't allow your children to play with guns, they may do so at other homes without your supervision. If you invite families from another culture or race into your home in a prejudiced neighborhood, your children may become the victims of teasing. There are no easy answers. True humility comes to us and our family when we realize how much we need God's grace and empowerment to live the Jesus way.

As you leave the pond, shimmering quietly in the late afternoon sun, reflect on some of these tips to help your family engage in faith issues related to shalom.

1. Help your children understand shalom by sharing stories about individuals who worked for peace, such as Mother Teresa, Martin Luther King Jr., Gandhi, or people you know. Read stories aloud from books such as Lehn's *Peace Be With You* (Faith & Life Press, 1980) or Battle's *Armed With Love* (Parthenon, 1973).

2. Share shalom faith with your family as you recycle, buy recycled goods, write letters of concern, and take steps to engage your family and others in caring for the environment. Teach your children to respect nature—God's beautiful creation—and put this respect into practice by what you say and do.

3. Recognize that truth telling is difficult. Give much time to talking about this with your children. Set up "What would you do?" situations. Help them understand how to ask for forgiveness when they have lied. As a parent, you need to be equally open to apologizing when you have broken their trust. Also note that telling perceived truth can be an inappropriate expression of biases. If your daughter tells another girl she is ugly, that is your daughter's perception and serves no purpose except to hurt the other's feelings.

4. Fights outside the family, especially at school, are on the rise. Because of your children's defenseless stance, other children may make them the objects of taunting and bullying. First, teach skills that don't antagonize or escalate conflict. If other steps fail, resort to lessons in nonviolent self-protection, such as karate.

For review and response

Recap

1. Shalom is not passive; it is a positive force that actively works toward God's intended purpose, the transformation of the world.

2. Shalom cannot be separated from justice because oppression, discrimination, and abuse are anti-shalom.

3. Shalom is not a concept; it is a relational reality central to one's profession of faith. Shalom is more than talk; it is a way of life.

4. Open your home to those deemed powerless. Provide toys and books that demonstrate concepts such as acceptance, understanding, and sharing across the lines of race, gender, age, and ability. Your child will soon assume that such openness is an essential ingredient of faith.

5. The greatest cause of disharmony in our global community is war and revolution.

6. One shalom concern is environmental. Our ecosystem is disrupted by users rather than keepers of the earth.

7. A shalom concern is the influence of violence, sexism, and bias on television and the ways commercials focus on immediate gratification, half-truths, and false promises.

8. There are many reasons for family conflict. Some have to do with power issues, and others are normal growing edges as the child exerts more independence.

What then shall we do?

1. Lack of outer and inner quiet in our society works against harmony and reflection. Help your children discover the significance of quiet moments. Share how Jesus often went to a quiet place. Announce a quiet play or book time. Set the timer for one minute multiplied by the age of the child for the appropriate attention span. Or make up quiet games during which everyone talks in a whisper. Share God's creation by standing together and quietly looking into the deep center of a flower or gazing at a sunset or the leaves of a houseplant. Plan vacations and expose your children to quiet woods where you and they listen for a bird's song, sit quietly beside a gurgling brook, silently watch small insects at work, and lie on your backs and look for faces in the clouds.

2. Family conflict is normal. But ongoing, unresolved conflict indicates that individual needs are not being met. Evaluate how you resolve conflict. Help your children negoti-

ate and respect each other's space and needs. Check your own feelings. Impatient, insecure parents may find it hard to be loving and nurturing or may even emotionally distance themselves from their children. Children learn readily that if they can't get positive attention, there are ways of getting negative attention.

3. Read the life of Jesus according to the Gospels. Underline passages that reinforce Jesus' emphasis on shalom as a faith lifestyle. For further guidance, read McGinnis's *Parenting for Peace and Justice* (Orbis, 1993).

4. Set a room divider in a corner to create a quiet space. On a small table, place a Bible, Bible story book, and other books. Children (depending on ages) may withdraw here to read, pray, think, or just be by themselves for a brief time. Parents escape here for brief prayer or reflection. You model faith for your children when they see you pray, read Scripture, or meditate.

5. Some parents lack inner harmony because they are still engaged in their own child-parent conflict engendered by longstanding hurt. Emotions sometimes govern our behaviors. If undealt with, we may unconsciously do the same things we disliked in our parents. Identify your issues and make peace with your past. If you can't manage it on your own, seek professional help.

For family

Family time

1. *Quiet thoughts.* Talk about how our minds race when we're always busy and don't take time to think about God, good thoughts, or ideas. Once a week, say grace after the meal and follow with a two- or three-minute time (longer for older children) for quiet thoughts. Provide crayons and

paper for those who want to doodle their thinking on paper. Take turns sharing quiet thoughts.

2. *Turf definitions.* Many conflicts arise in families because turf issues are not clarified or respected. Participate in the following for several weeks:

Personal and general space: Each person needs places in the home defined as personal space. On newsprint, draw a large blueprint of your home. Have each family member draw a square around areas that are his or her personal space, like a place at the table, a space in their room, etc. Personal space must be respected by others and not taken over or intruded on without permission. Color in all other areas to represent general space. Here, everyone is responsible, and no one can claim it as their own. Discuss what it takes in your home to respect each other's needs in general space (example, watching TV). Read Romans 12:18.

Possession space: By age four, most children understand sharing. But each person needs to have some things they are not required to share and some items they are willing to share but permission from another is required. Give each family member a sheet where they list or draw pictures in each category. Talk about these and add or change as needed. The more mature, the higher the self-esteem, the more capable a child is of sharing. Ask them to identify items they are willing to share with family members without permission being required. Make up some sharing role plays, such as "Tony got a new bike for his birthday and John wants to ride it." Now what?

Time space: Have each family member draw the face of a clock and color in those blocks of time that belong to school, to family responsibilities, and to self. Talk about what happens when self time is scheduled for piano practice, but Dad insists you set the table. Or self time says you can watch TV, but your sister's clock has the same schedule. Family time says you are to sweep the walk, but your friend comes over. What can you do? Family issues change often, so I suggest you frequently engage in this discussion. Read Romans 12:16a.

3. *Peacemaker collage.* Read Matthew 5:9. Talk about ways family members can be peacemakers at home, school, and in the world. Provide magazines, cut out pictures of peacemaking activities, and glue onto a sheet of newspaper from the recycling bin. Each person shares his or her contribution. Close with a litany.

Parent: When someone in the family argues,
Family: Jesus, help me to be a peacemaker.
Child: When my friends are mean to each other,
Family: Jesus, help me to be a peacemaker.
Child: When children at school or people at work fight,
Family: Jesus, help me to be a peacemaker.
Parent: Where there is hatred and war,
All: Jesus, help our family to be peacemakers. Amen.

4. *Another way.* Assess media as your family discusses shalom.

Videos: View videos such as "Gandhi" or "The Karate Kid" (or find more recent ones) which tell of nonviolent ways of resolving conflict. Discuss what this has to do with Jesus' teachings about being peacemakers or about turning the other cheek (Matthew 5:9, 39-40).

Television: View programs and cartoons. Observe violent behavior, put-downs, and other demeaning acts towards others. Think of the Jesus way and then come up with alternative endings to the plot.

Newspaper: Select conflict stories or items from your daily paper and discuss what tactics people used to resolve conflict. Discuss or act out alternative endings.

5. *Multicultural foods*. Help your children appreciate and enjoy the diversity of God's people in our society, which include the Native People, African-American, Chinese, Haitian, Vietnamese, ethnic German, and many other groups. Identify people of diverse backgrounds in your neighborhood; get to know them, their customs, and foods. Share or find recipes and make one (such as the Navajo Fry Bread recipe on this page). Share your faith by affirming that we are all equal, all God's creation.

Navajo Fry Bread

2 cups/500 ml. flour
1/2 teaspoon/2 ml. salt
2 teaspoons/10 ml. baking powder
1/2 cup/125 ml. powdered milk

Mix dry ingredients. Stir in warm water to make a firm dough. Let rise two hours. Shape into small balls and flatten into large, thin circles. Make a thimble-sized hole in the middle. Deep-fry, drain on paper towels, and sprinkle with powdered sugar.

Celebrate the family

Celebrate Earth Day. The earth, God's beautiful creation, is a delicate place to live. Each year an international Earth Day is proclaimed, but you can establish your own date. Think of ways your family can celebrate shalom by caring for the earth. An idea: Dip donut-shaped cookies (or small donuts) in beaten eggwhite, roll in bird seed, attach bright yarn, and hang outdoors for your feathered friends.

An idea for a family night activity

Neighborhood soup. Soup makes a fine meal even finer if shared. To a pot of water add salt, a meat bone, bay leaf, and parsley. Invite your children to access the fridge or cupboard and add items of their choice. Invite friends to come over and bring a fresh or canned vegetable to add to the neighborhood soup. While the soup simmers, ask everyone to share a story. Or watch a video. While eating, have everyone tell what he or she added to the soup. After-meal options: (1) Read and discuss John 6:9-13. Talk about God's surprises when we share. Suggest and discuss the possibility of a neighbor group that will gather food items for needy families. Ask the children for their ideas. (2) Play parlor games that involve everyone.

For study

Search the Scriptures

"Now may the Lord of peace ... give you peace at all times and in every way" (2 Thessalonians 3:16a).

What is your definition of "all times and in every way"?

The early church frequently refers to a God of peace who bestows peace and encourages believers to live in peace. 1 Peter 3:11 says the believer must seek and pursue peace. How can peace be both bestowed and pursued?

Discuss the questions

1. Peace is more than the absence of war. Describe your view of a society at peace. Share your understanding of a family where shalom reigns. What does it take?

2. If God is love and a God of peace (harmony), how is this evidenced by the way you share your faith with your children and the world around you? Give some examples.

Engage in group response

1. Select New Testament references to peace from a concordance. Each person selects a verse to read aloud. Sub-

stitute "shalom" for "peace." Reflect what this verse means for your family. Lay newsprint on a table. Each member uses a marker to draw a symbol of the verse's meaning for her or him without lifting the marker. When finished, the next person continues the line, drawing a symbol that best clarifies her or his verse's significance. When finished, you'll have a shared symbol of your group's understanding of shalom. Discuss the individual and total contributions.

2. Before you conclude this session, read the following prayer in unison. Then read it again and substitute the word "me" for "us."

World Peace Prayer: Lead us from death to life, from falsehood to truth. Lead us from despair to hope, from fear to trust. Lead us from hate to love, from war to peace. Let peace fill our hearts, our world, our universe. Amen.

Chapter 13

Friends in the Meadow

How the Support of a Faith Community Strengthens the Family

....

In pastures green

You're almost home. The last half-mile leads through a meadow where green grass intermingles with patches of wildflowers exploding in every hue and shape. The late rains have brought out this plethora. I recall a 1960s spring in southwestern Kansas. Winters and springs had been extremely dry for two years, and suddenly one downpour after another spilled across the land, bringing to life multitudes of toads and other beings awakened from their dusty habitats. On our way to an old ranch, we wound through meadows bursting with blossoms, a wild profusion of color, much as you are seeing here. Seeds, patiently waiting through drought, had sprung to life in response to long-hoped-for showers.

There is joy in the glow of color splashed across a mead-ow canvas. You want to gather the colors in armfuls, bring them into the shelters, and call out, "Look what has happened to the seed!" The faith you share with your children is much like that. You plant your seeds, year in and year out, but God provides the rains. Slowly, sometimes suddenly, you see life emerging and the many colors of faith response growing here and there. It takes much faith to have faith. It takes much patience to share faith with your children. It takes much faith to believe that God will touch their lives—not necessarily in the way yours was touched, but in ways that make their God experience real for them.

Soon your young ones will be teenagers, and at times you will wonder whether anything rubbed off. Be assured, here and there you will begin to see blossoms. In their 20s and 30s and 40s or even later (with some you may never know), they come to you, share their faith with you, and express appreciation for what you gave to them from the first day. And then you remember how the innocent faith of their child-hood, even the turbulent struggles of youth, touched and test-ed your faith, pushing you toward depth and growth. It may not always happen exactly this way, but in the thought lies the hope and prayer of every parent. You plant your seeds care-fully and wait. The rest is grace.

Your young ones are calling. Not too far away you see people running toward you: adults, children, and even the family dog. "Hello, hello," they call. Soon you are together, laughing, greeting, hugging. "Why didn't you tell us you were going?" one says. "We would have come with you." As you look back on the day, you realize how different many aspects of it would have been had they accompanied you. You sense the value and support of those who care about you. These are friends you can depend on in good times and bad. They'll be with you no matter what.

Learning the value of support groups, of the caring of one's own family and the church family, is critical to being the family of God. As you walk toward the house, you talk about your day. You reflect on the helping hands needed to support your family, to encourage you in your faith journey and in sharing of that faith with your children.

Many family problems in our society are due to isolation. Single parents try to raise their children in an urban setting with few outside contacts. Moved to a new setting because of a job transfer, families feel shaken and uprooted. Blended families with spouses frequently from different backgrounds try to negotiate a new family shape with few models or little counsel.

Today, communities where next of kin are close at hand and can be depended on for companionship and support are an exception rather than a rule. Yet the human is created for being with others not only during the early developmental years but also throughout life. How do we attain relationships that give us the needed support, caring, and insights for our personal growth? Who are those unique others who can help us understand ways to guide, relate to, and share our faith with our children?

Why do families need more support today than ever before?

Our technological era has produced a mechanistic view of the human, where worth is based on productivity. The increase in crime by and upon children is frightening. Fear of strangers, sexual abuse, kidnapping, and murder cause stress for parents who worry when children are out of sight. In the early 1970s, our three-year-old and his friend could roam the five-acre woods behind our house; today I would not permit it.

Social problems multiply as population increases and rapid urbanization changes the face of our society. The gun-toting mentality of the old west has not yet been replaced by civilized, cultured behavior. Violence begets violence. Parents and children feel pressured to accept lifestyles in conflict with those learned in simpler, less confusing times. An increasing number of children are sexually active, try drugs, or are faced with pregnancy. Gangs are spreading into suburbs and small towns. Families worry about security. Children are taught not to answer the door or phone when home alone. TV brings the whole world to our doorstep every evening, and children view terror and tragedy to the point of becoming immune.

Families not only struggle with fear but also with feeling overwhelmed. They are faced with innumerable options, to the point where children may want to try many things without putting their heart into anything. Sometimes it's easier to let someone else make the decisions or choose the easiest path. My eight-year-old piano student moans, "I have no time to play."

These are only a few of the issues families face. There are many more, such as job security, unexpected medical bills, traumas in the community or home, mental illness, disabilities, and so on. At a time when families face many possibilities, family problems that cut across social, cultural, and economic lines intensify. Many adults don't have the skills, stamina, or insight to logically solve problems, to negotiate or to compromise. Faith may seem unrelated to the issues at hand. That's why families need much support.

Where do you find support if you're a single parent?

Single parents face an incredible task. They may be single by choice (adopting or birthing a child) or through divorce or death of spouse. Each situation is different. They may be teenagers or older. Today, a significant number of grandparents, often single, are raising their grandchildren. These single parents come from suburbia, rural communities, and the inner city. They have much in common. In most cases, the single parent is the primary provider who returns from work and assumes full responsibility for parenting and home and yard care. The single parent has little time for self, reflection, or social life. An elderly grandparent may face all this plus a fixed income and limited energy.

Whatever the situation, the bare bones facts are that one person carries the full load and responsibility of parenting. There is no one to blame and no escape. One makes decisions without the benefit of a spouse's perspective and must accept the consequences of decisions. So how does a single parent experience and communicate faith?

The primary need of a single parent is dependable, caring support. Find a church where this can occur. Attend retreats, workshops, and so on, for single parents. Support groups for divorced parents and grief groups are equally as important. Parents that never married face particular isolation and bias. Talk with your pastor about the need for such groups.

In a caring group, you can share your struggles and develop a faith community where you help each other. Take turns providing child care for each other to give you a chance for renewal. Also, find a confidante you can depend on, someone with whom you can consult.

The church must back single parents and help alleviate stress so that these parents can find time and energy to share their own faith with their young ones. Invite them for meals. Include them in activities. Give a hand. Be sensitive to a grandparent raising children. She or he has a wealth of faith experience stories, but may need physical support. Include these children in some of your activities. Model a mother or father role for those children who have none.

Can you find support from a significant other?

The best gift parents can give their children is love for and support of each other. Sharing faith becomes difficult when spouses are embroiled in long-standing conflict, misunderstanding, and lack of respect. Couples need to develop skills in negotiating their roles and relationships so that both can come out feeling like winners. Being open and honest in communication, trying to hear the other person without placing judgment, and recognizing the "otherness" of that person are all critical to mutuality and growth.

A marriage goes through many stages. If each spouse doesn't grow accordingly, conflict is bound to ensue. To understand your spouse more fully, recognize that adults have different personalities just as your children do. The oppositeness which attracted you before marriage may become the point of tension as you unconsciously try to make him or her over to be like you. The more opposite personalities or cultural differences, the harder a couple has to work at the relationship. That's why couples need to spend time talking, praying, and sharing. The potential for growth is enormous.

To retain community in marriage, spouses need to reassess the shape of their marriage periodically and identify shifts or changes that have occurred. According to Scanzoni in *Men, Women and Change* (McGraw Hill, 1976), there are various shapes of marriage: the traditional, where one is in charge (usually male); the complementary, where one spouse (usually female) enhances the profession of the other; the working couple, where the job of one spouse (usually female) is considered less significant than the other; and the egalitarian marriage, where both are equally responsible as breadwinners, homemakers, and caretakers of children. There are numerous adaptations. Any shape can work if understood and negotiated. But if one spouse becomes dissatisfied or out-grows a role, conflict or distancing occurs.

The same type of sharing needs to take place between spouses on faith issues. Respect the faith (or lack of it) in your spouse, and set aside your judgments. Recognize, as with your children, that faith is a gift. God graces you, and together you try to find mutual areas of growth and understanding. Your attempt to be a faith partnership will benefit your children.

Although the focus here is on younger nuclear families, recognize that an increasing number of couples are having their children after thirty or forty. With new fertility proce-dures, that age is escalating. Grandparents or older relatives are also raising children, and some older couples are adopting children. The discussions and activities in this chapter (and book) need to be interpreted and adapted to your particular situation. Underneath it all are the basic questions: "How do I create Christian community, and how do I share my faith with the children that God has entrusted to me?"

How is the family a support system within itself?

When a family spends time together, engages in various activities and discussions (as recommended in this book), and faith is shared freely, a support community is formed. Your task is to guide your children step-by-step through faith and life experiences toward independence.

Blended families face some challenges different from nuclear families. Families with different values and back-grounds come together. In a blended family, at least one group of children will be moved, age-groupings may change, and turf issues may surface. Some children resent the new parent and even sabotage the relationship. These families need to spend a great deal of time together in activities, talking out feelings, and respecting the needs of individuals and the space needed. Usually blending means coping with an instant larger family, agreeing on child-rearing approaches, and a mutual way of dealing with faith issues.

Blending a family takes time. Spouses also blend their faith experiences, approaches to the children, ways of sharing, and many other aspects of life together. Encourage your children to see this as possibility for new growth. Find books for the children to read. Browse in your denominational bookstore for resources, and be intentional about the way you build this new family and family shape. As in any marriage, you and your spouse need to spend much time in discussion, planning, and prayer.

How can we create an extended family?

Churches today try to create an extended family. But often these families see each other only once a week and have little in common. Mobility and rapid change work against this sense of community, particularly in urban centers. If you are committed to your denomination, your family may find itself driving long distances for worship. Your children may react against going because their peers are not there, and you may find yourself a stranger among strangers.

Withdrawing reinforces the estrangement and prolongs the isolation. Become involved. Participate in intergenerational activities. Join a group, or find out who your children are relating to and get together with these families. Time will tell whether the relationships mesh and whether this could be the source for a family support group. Don't expect relationships to happen by themselves. You must be intentional and ready to open your home. Don't wait for someone else to contact you. Hospitality is a biblical injunction (Romans 12:13, Hebrews 13:2) and models inclusiveness to your children.

When you think of the church as a support community, don't limit yourself to one age-group, family shape, or family style. It is natural that couples with children want to be with others like them. Blended families congregate toward each other. Single parents feel they have more in common with other single parents. That is all fine and good, but the community of Jesus Christ is rich in diversity. Society is often segregated by age, gender, marital status, race, and culture. But the church represents transformation. The power of the Spirit supersedes barriers and breaks down walls that normally distance people from each other. Your family is enriched by experiencing community with people of different ages, situations, and cultures.

Finding local community support and relationships becomes more difficult, especially in urban centers. In rural areas, small towns, and even older suburbs, it is easier to engage in neighboring with others of faith. In developing highly mobile suburbs, which attract young families because of safety and neighborhood schools, community becomes more difficult. We've lived in our present neighborhood for three years. During that time, five families around us have moved out and three have moved in. Often they don't know anyone. In smaller or older communities, it was common for some in the neighborhood to welcome newcomers. But now we leave it to organizations, such as Welcome Wagon.

How do you establish a neighborhood? How do you find families of faith to share with? You need to begin by assertively reaching out. If you've moved in, watch for neighbors in their yard or on the sidewalk. Walk over and introduce yourself. Welcome newcomers. Attend school functions. Encourage your children to invite friends over. Get acquainted with the parents. You may eventually find families of faith with whom you want to meet regularly for social and for faith support reasons.

Feelings of belonging in the family, church, and community enrich the faith growth of your children. You cannot go it alone. Children will flourish and blossom in an environment where inclusiveness is practiced and the helping, healing faith community stands beside you. As they observe others, children will recognize the many splendors of faith, and they will grow through the witness of the larger family to which you have committed yourself.

Travel tips

You have walked for a day through the woods. Now the walk is over and you are home. You will make this journey again and again, but it will be a different excursion each time. Your growing children are constantly developing and changing. The shape of the family may change. You may have other travel companions. The woods, the winds, and the weather also move in their own rhythm. The seasons shape the moods of the wild. Your next walk, though somewhat familiar, will present you with unexpected adventure. Therein lies the excitement and surprise of life with your children as you continue the journey of faith sharing. For today, you've had enough. It's time to assimilate and reflect. Review the many travel tips in this book. Where will you go from here?

For review and response

Recap

1. Many family problems in our society are due to isolation. Yet the human is created for being with others during the early developmental years and throughout life.

2. Many adults don't have the skills, stamina, or insight to solve problems through negotiation or compromise. Faith may seem unrelated to the issues at hand. That's why families need much support.

3. Single parents face an incredible task. The primary need of a single parent is dependable, caring support.

4. The best gift parents can give their children is love for and support of each other. Couples need to develop many skills in negotiating their roles and relationships so that both can come out feeling like winners.

5. When a family (including a blended family) spends time together, engages in various activities and discussions, and faith is shared freely, a support community is formed.

6. When you think of the church as a support community, don't limit yourself to one age-group, family shape, or family style.

7. Feelings of belonging in the family, church, and community enrich the faith growth of your children. You cannot go it alone. Children will flourish and blossom in an environment where inclusiveness is practiced and the helping, healing faith community stands beside you.

What then shall we do?

1. Find several families with whom you feel comfortable. Make sure to include single persons, single-parent families, and multicultural families. Make a commitment to spend time together on a regular basis. Once a month engage in an informal worship service. Become a caring group. Help each other out, bring in food during times of crisis, visit each other in hospitals, or engage in joint service projects. By involving others to share faith with your family, you expand your children's horizons and give them the benefit of broader support and faith witness.

2. Review the *Recaps* in this book. Give special attention to the chapters that focus on the moral and faith stages of children. Through a spoken or written prayer, make a commitment to the Lord to grow in your faith. Ask the Spirit to

make you sensitive to how, where, and when you can most appropriately share your faith with your children.

For family

Family time

1. *Car sing-along.* I have fond memories of our family singing during travels. Singing together bonded us and left behind a heritage of hymns. Begin when your children are small. Sing their favorite songs and yours. Children learn readily. Soon they will sing along as you travel. You share your faith by singing favorite hymns again and again until they are memorized. Your children can then sing them anytime, anywhere.

2. *Develop empathy.* A word that characterizes Jesus is "compassion." When we build community only with those who are like us, we miss something. Open your home to families who have a disabled member, or learn about mental illness and how it affects families (contact your nearest mental health center for information). Experience what it's like to be disabled. Try to read or carry on a conversation with the radio blaring (persons with schizophrenia may hear constant intrusive voices in their minds). Open a door without your hands. Eat your dinner blindfolded. Watch your favorite TV show with cotton in your ears. Take turns climbing stairs with crutches. Visit a mall with one member in a wheelchair and watch people's reactions.

3. *Friendship hands.* Talk about God's families who live around the world and the many nationalities and races in our society. Have everyone draw around their hands several times on poster board, and cut them out. Leave about 2 inches/5 centimeters wrist length above each hand. Ask each one to decide which countries their hands will represent. With a marker, write the name of the country on the

hand; color the hand according to a skin color commonly found there. (Be aware that numerous skin colors are represented in the United States and Canada.) Glue the fingers of one hand over the wrist area of the next one, forming a circle. When done, glue both ends together. Gather around the Friendship Hands. Note that the circle represents unity and caring. Take turns praying for families in these countries.

4. *Seed community.* Plant oat or wheat seeds (grass is an option) in a bowl or planter. As the grain grows, discuss about how we develop, how we learn to love Jesus more each day, and how family and church are like the seedlings growing together. At Easter, lay your colored eggs in the bed of grain (grasses) and use as a table centerpiece. At Christmastime, place a candle in the center or place bright, colored balls in the bowl. At Valentine's Day, glue a toothpick between two paper hearts and place in the planter. Talk about meanings for each seasonal centerpiece.

5. *Word collage prayer.* This idea can be used repeatedly as a means of sharing your faith because the blanks you and your children fill in may change according to your situations. The basic thrust is to guide your children toward understanding and appreciating the support of community. Also, this prayer thanks God for the faith, influence, and help of various communities from family to church. Appoint or ask various members to fill in the blanks when you pause in your reading. All participate in the response.

Parent: On days when I feel _____, I talk to _____ in my family.
Family: Thank-you, God, for our family.
Parent: When I feel _____ at (school, work, or play), I can _____.
Family: Thank-you, God, for friends.
Parent: When I go to church, I _____.
Family: Thank-you, God, for the church.

Parent: With God, the church, friends, and family, we are never _____.
All: Thank-you, God. Thank-you, God. Amen.

Celebrate the family

Celebrate a big happy birthday! Build community in the family by making each one feel special. Celebrate each member's birthday for several days. Plan activities (excuse the birthday child) you will engage in for days prior to the event. Consider these suggestions: (1) Serve the person's favorite meal or dessert. (2) Each one blows up a balloon and writes a special message on it. Give it to him or her. (3) Make a giant family birthday card and deliver it days before the birthday. (4) From magazines, cut words or pictures that describe this person and present them. (5) Make a surprise birthday banner and hang it on his or her door. (6) Cut footsteps from construction paper. Lay a trail throughout the house leading to an early gift. (7) In advance, ask grandparents or a significant other to record a birthday story, preferably the story of a year or party when they reached the same age as your child.

An idea for a family night activity

Friends around the world. Ask your pastor to help you find names of families in other countries, possibly members in your denomination's mission churches or a missionary family. Discuss God's love for the world (John 3:16). Share how we are all parts of a larger body. Like legs, arms, eyes, and so on, we belong together (1 Corinthians 12:12). Decide which family you will write to. Each family member writes a few lines and signs his or her name. Younger ones dictate while you write. Add a photo or drawing of your family.

For study

Search the Scriptures

"The body is a unit, though it is made up of many parts; and though all its parts are many, they form one body. So it is with Christ" (1 Corinthians 12:12).

How do body parts support each other? How does this relate to the church as a supporting, caring community?

How would you explain this verse to your children?

Discuss the questions

1. Who are the members of your extended family? Relatives? Single persons? Other families? What age-groups are represented? Cultures? What do you like about your present situation, and what would you like to change?

2. How do you find community and support in the church?

Engage in group response

1. Which of the aspects of community discussed in this chapter are most important to you? Discuss.

3. Where do you go from here? What will the nature and future support of this group be for each of you? Discuss and come to some conclusions.

Closing reflection

1. Read Philippians 4:4-8.

2. Make or buy a huge cookie and write the words FAITH, HOPE, and LOVE on it with a frosting tip. Pass it around and ask each one to break a piece and hold it. Before eating, read together "We commit ourselves and our families to life lived in faith, hope, and love, believing we walk in the

company of many believers and the presence of God."

3. Make a prayer commitment to one another. In advance, write the names of all participants on slips of paper and tie onto a long piece of yarn about six feet apart. Roll into a ball. Pass the ball (unwind as you pass). Each person unties a name and passes it on. Note that the yarn represents the circle of community. The names are a call to pray for each other.

Appendix A

Erikson's Developmental Tasks: Emotional Development

Age	Polarities	Achievement	Questions	Danger if Not Accomplished
0-2	Trust vs. Mistrust	I can trust people	Can I trust my parents (caretakers) to meet my needs? Will I be fed, cared for, kept comfortable?	The world and people are undependable. There is no meaning in life.
2-4	Autonomy vs. Shame and Doubt	I can discriminate in a world of right and wrong	Can I make appropriate choices between acceptable and unacceptable behavior (symbolized by toilet training in Western culture)? Can I still feel good about myself if I experience shame and doubt?	I need to be right. Precocious rigid conscience; compulsiveness, inflexibility, overcontrol.
4-6	Initiative vs. Guilt	I can act.	Can I act, express initiative, be aggressive, use my muscles within set limits? Must I feel guilty if I overstep? If I am indeed guilty, will I be forgiven?	Inner guilt over goals and actions. Fear of losing control of one's actions. Self-doubt.
6-11/12	Industry vs. Inferiority	I can do things well, be masterful.	Can I perform, be skillful, learn to read and do math, use tools, manipulate?	Feelings of inadequacy, inferiority. Workaholic syndrome (work is the only source of meaning in life).
11/12-18/21	Identity vs. Role Confusion	I am me, a male or female	(This stage offers a chance to regroup.) Have I successfully learned my first lessons: trust, autonomy, initiative, industry? If there are weak spots, how can I recoup my losses? What does it mean to be a man or a woman? Is it safe to be me—or must I be like everyone else?	Role confusion. Confused self-image. Overidentification with a group.
Young Adulthood	Intimacy vs. Isolation	I can give myself to others.	If I know who I am, can I give myself away? Can I be committed even if sacrifice or compromise may be necessary?	Loss of self-dignity. Fear of reaching out to others.
Adulthood	Generativity vs. Stagnation	I can be creative and caring	Can I be productive, do satisfying work, establish and guide a new generation of people, make a purposeful life? Am I at peace with authority so that I can both accept it and exercise it?	Stagnation; loss of creativity. Self-indulgence.
Maturity	Integrity vs. Despair	I can be complete.	Can I accept my life and be satisfied with what I have done?	Inability to retire from formal work. Fear of death.

Used by permission from *Upon These Doorposts* by Marlene Kropf, Bertha Fast Harder, and Linea Geiser (Evangel Press, Faith & Life Press, and Mennonite Publishing House, 1980), p. 24.

Appendix B

The Spiritual Dimensions of Faith

THE CIRCLE OF FAITH

Used by permission from *Upon These Doorposts* by Marlene Kropf, Bertha Fast Harder, and Linea Geiser (Evangel Press, Faith & Life Press, and Mennonite Publishing House, 1980), p. 26.

Appendix C

Comparative Chart of Developmental Theories (Patterns) of Growth

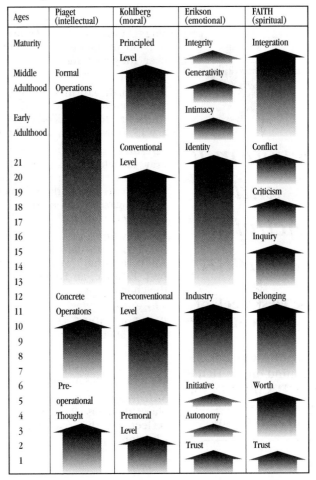

Ages	Piaget (intellectual)	Kohlberg (moral)	Erikson (emotional)	FAITH (spiritual)
Maturity		Principled Level	Integrity	Integration
Middle Adulthood	Formal Operations		Generativity	
Early Adulthood			Intimacy	
		Conventional Level	Identity	Conflict
21				
20				
19				Criticism
18				
17				
16				Inquiry
15				
14				
13				
12	Concrete Operations	Preconventional Level	Industry	Belonging
11				
10				
9				
8				
7				
6	Pre-operational Thought		Initiative	Worth
5				
4		Premoral Level	Autonomy	
3				
2			Trust	Trust
1				

Used by permission from *Upon These Doorposts* by Marlene Kropf, Bertha Fast Harder, and Linea Geiser (Evangel Press, Faith & Life Press, and Mennonite Publishing House, 1980), p. 30.

Appendix D

Devotional and Activity Calendar for Advent

Devotional and Activity Calendar:

The First Week of Advent

During this week, focus your mind on the HOPE and ANTICIPATION you feel as you wait for the coming of Jesus.

Sunday
Light the first Advent candle and sing "O Come, O Come, Emmanuel." It is an invitation. Invite someone over for games and refreshments.

Monday
Read Isaiah 9:6. In some Scandinavian countries, people celebrate Christmas from December 13-January 13. How would you celebrate?

Tuesday
Pray for children and families in war-battered countries. Collect news items about these countries from magazines and make a "Prayer Reminder" collage.

Wednesday
Recite or read the carol "O Come, All Ye Faithful," written in France by J. F. Wade, an Englishman. Sing the chorus.

Thursday
Read Isaiah 40:1-5. Draw and color a picture about it. Share.

Friday
Plan to go Christmas shopping or see a Christmas movie tomorrow.

Saturday
Share thoughts about the day and reflect on the real meaning of Christmas.

Used by permission from *Christmas Everywhere* by Anne Neufeld Rupp (Educational Ministries, 1994), pp. 23-24.

Other Ideas

· Go for a "wonder walk." Pretend you are Mary and Joseph. Ask and talk about "wonder" questions like: "I wonder where Mary and Joseph slept on their long journey?" "I wonder what Mary and Joseph talked about?"

· Make a lantern. In the Philippines, families make brightly colored lanterns and walk outside. Invite other families. Make green and red lanterns and put on neighborhood parades.

· Design and make a HOPE banner.

· Make a creche, a French custom. Build excitement by adding a figure each night. Add the Christ child on Christmas Eve. (Carve extra figures, such as townspeople, from soap or soft wood.)

Devotional and Activity Calendar:

The Second Week of Advent

During this week, think about the message of the angels, "Glory to God in the highest, and on earth PEACE..." (Luke 2:14).

Sunday
Light the first and second Advent candles. Talk about what the wreath and the candle colors signify.

Monday
In 1879, Thomas Edison showed his light bulb in public for the first time. Three years later, electric lights decorated the first tree. Light your tree every evening from now on.

Tuesday
Read Micah 5:2. Try to make a four-line poem about this verse.

Wednesday
Christopher Columbus celebrated his first Christmas in the New World in 1492 and invited an Indian chief, ruler of Haiti, to be his guest. Talk about this and plan to invite a family for a meal this weekend.

Thursday
Pray for the families of the former U.S.S.R. Especially remember the children of Moscow and St. Petersburg.

Friday
Cut pictures from old cards and make a card that describes the real meaning of Christmas.

Saturday
In 1865, Philip Brooks, while visiting Palestine, rode through the Field of the Shepherds on Christmas Eve. This experience led him to write "O Little Town of Bethlehem." Sing the hymn.

Used by permission from *Christmas Everywhere* by Anne Neufeld Rupp (Educational Ministries, 1994), pp. 25-26.

Other Ideas

- Give each member of your family a gift certificate. List on each certificate something special that you do for that person this week.
- Spend time with someone who's alone, or invite him or her over to your house.
- Plan to give gifts of food, clothing, and money to persons in need.
- Martin Luther, the 16th-century reformer, loved celebrations as a child and later as a man. He used to carol with his friends. Some say he introduced the Christmas tree with candles to Germany. Stand around your tree and sing the German carol "O Tannenbaum" (O Christmas Tree).
- Design and make a PEACE banner.

Devotional and Activity Calendar:

The Third Week of Advent

This is a week for
REJOICING in anticipation
of Christmas. Share your
joy with others in what
you say and do.

Sunday
Light three candles (including the rose one). Read Phillippians 4:4-7.

Monday
Do a chore or favor for someone.

Tuesday
Make an ornament for your tree or give it to a friend.

Wednesday
Invite someone who lives alone to dinner.

Thursday
Make someone smile.

Friday
Say a prayer for peace.

Saturday
Call someone you rarely see.

Used by permission from *Christmas Everywhere* by Anne Neufeld Rupp (Educational Ministries, 1994), pp. 27-28.

Other Ideas

- Decorate your house and tree. Candles, lights, and ever-green boughs can help express the joy of the coming of Jesus. Make ornaments for your tree; invite friends and neighbors to help you hang the ornaments.
- Present or attend a pageant. Attend a pageant put on by your church or local school. Or, you and your family or friends can dramatize a story from the Bible for others to see. (For example, use Matthew 1:18-25 or Luke 2:1-20.)
- Help prepare your church. Offer to help decorate your church or to assist with other details that must be taken care of before Christmas Eve.
- "Count your blessings." Make a list of the most joyous things that have happened to you and your family this year. Offer a prayer of thanksgiving to God. Read Matthew 6:19-34.

Devotional and Activity Calendar:

The Fourth Week of Advent

These last days before Christmas are a time of rejoicing. Share JOY with others. Ponder the Magi, "When they saw the star, they were overjoyed." (Matthew 2:10), NIV

Sunday
Light all four Advent candles. Read Isaiah 60:1-2. Attend a concert or listen to a recording of G. F. Handel's oratoria "The Messiah."

Monday
Each family member chooses a carol, and the whole family sings.

Tuesday
Pray for families in the Middle East and Australia.

Wednesday
Read Luke 2:1-20.

Thursday
Spend time thinking about the gifts given to you — life, faith, family, and friends. Thank God for these gifts.

Friday
Listen to instrumental Christmas music or make your own.

Saturday
Think about the New Year and write one resolution.

Used by permission from *Christmas Everywhere* by Anne Neufeld Rupp (Educational Ministries, 1994), pp. 29-30.

Other Ideas

- Attend a pageant, or you and your family can dramatize Luke 2:1-20 for others to see. Serve cookies and punch.
- On Christmas Eve, light all candles on your wreath. Place the Christ child in the manger. Stand around the creche and sing the American hymn "Away in a Manger." Find as many candles as you can in the house, bring them to the room where you are gathered, and light them all. Listen to recorded carols or sing "Joy to the World" by Isaac Watts.
- Phone someone to wish them a "Merry Christmas."
- Design and make a JOY banner.
- Roll a glue-covered glass in glitter and make a "Giving Glass." On Christmas Eve, parents designate an amount each member may give to a need in your church, country, or overseas. Each one shares her/his choice, writes it on paper, and drops it into the glass. Parents send out the designated checks later.

Bibliography

Bates, Ames, and Francis Ilge. *The Gesell Institute's Child Behavior*. New York: Harper and Row, 1955.

Bates, Marilyn, and David Keirsey. *Please Understand Me*. Del Mar, California: Prometheus Nemesis Books, 1978.

Anderson, Ray, and Dennis Guernsey. *On Being Family*. Grand Rapids, Michigan: William Eerdman Publishing Company, 1985.

Bach, Richard. *Jonathan Livingston Seagull*. Macmillan, 1970.

Bernheim, Lewine and Beale. *The Caring Family, Living with Chronic Mental Illness*. New York: Random House, 1982.

Bridges, William. *Transitions*. Reading, Massachusetts: Addison-Wesley Publishing Company, 1980.

Briggs, Dorothy Corkille. *Your Child's Self-Esteem*. Garden City, New York: Doubleday and Company (Dolphin Books), 1975.

Cully, Iris. *Christian Child Development*. Harper and Row, 1979.

Davidson, Linda and Robert, editors. *Church Educator*. 165 Plaza Drive, Prescott, Arizona 86303, 1987-1994.

Dodson, Fitzhugh. *How to Parent*. New York: New American Library, Inc., 1971.

Drescher, John M. *When Your Child.* Scottdale, Pennsylvania: Herald Press, 1986.

Furnish, Dorothy. *Exploring the Bible with Children.* Nashville: Abingdon Press, 1975.

Geiser, Linea, Bertha Fast Harder, and Marlene Kropf. *Upon These Doorposts.* Nappanee, Indiana: Evangel Press; Newton, Kansas: Faith & Life Press; and Scottdale, Pennsylvania: Mennonite Publishing House, 1980.

Gesell, Arnold. *Youth, the Years from Ten to Sixteen.* Harper and Row, 1956.

Gesell, Arnold. *The Child from Five to Ten.* Harper and Row, 1977.

Gesell, Arnold. *The First Five Years.* Harper and Row, 1940.

Gibran, Kahlil. *The Prophet.* New York: Knopf, 1965.

Ginott, Haim G. *Between Parent and Child.* New York: Avon Books, 1965.

Heller, David. *Talking to Your Child about God.* New York: Berkley Publishing Company, 1994.

Hersey, Paul and Kenneth H. Blanchard. *The Family Game.* Reading, Massachusetts: Addison-Wesley Publishing Company, 1978.

Hoffman, Edward. *Visions of Innocence.* Boston: Shambhala Publications, 1992.

Hover, Margot. *A Happier Family.* Mystic, Connecticut: Twenty-Third Publications, 1978.

Klink, Johanna. *Your Child and Religion.* Richmond, Virginia: John Knox Press, 1972.

Kubler-Ross, Elizabeth. *On Death and Dying.* New York: Macmillan, 1969.

Larson, Roland S. and Doris E. *Values and Faith.* Minneapolis: Winston Press, 1976.

Lehn, Cornelia. *Children and Faith.* Newton, Kansas: Faith & Life Press, 1993.

McGinnis, James and Kathleen. *Parenting for Peace and Justice, Ten Years Later.* Maryknoll, New York: Orbis Books, 1993.

Patterson, Gerald R. *Families.* Champaign, Illinois: Research Press, 1975.

Phillips, J. B. *Your God Is Too Small.* Phoenix Press, 1986.

Rupp, Anne Neufeld. *Christmas Everywhere.* Prescott, Arizona: Education Ministries, 1994.

Satir, Virginia. *Peoplemaking.* Palo Alto, California: Science and Behavior Books, 1972.

Scanzoni, Letha and John. *Men, Women and Change.* McGraw Hill, 1976.

Shedd, Charlie. *Promises to Peter.* Waco, Texas: Word, 1970.

Simon, Sydney. *Helping Your Child Find Values to Live By.* New York: Simon and Schuster, 1991.

Simon, Sydney. *Strengthening Stepfamilies.* Circle Pines, Minnesota: American Guidance Service, 1986.

Westerhoff, John III. *Will Our Children Have Faith?* New York: Seabury Press, 1976.

Resources for Children

Battle, Gerald N. *Armed With Love* (Stories of the Disciples). Nashville: Parthenon, 1973.

Cooner, Donna, and Kim Simons (illustrator). *The World God Made.* Dallas: Word Publishing, 1994.

Lehn, Cornelia. *I Heard Good News Today.* Newton, Kansas: Faith & Life Press, 1983.

Lehn, Cornelia. *God Keeps His Promises.* Newton, Kansas: Faith & Life Press, 1970.

Lehn, Cornelia. *Peace Be With You.* Newton, Kansas: Faith & Life Press, 1980.

Love, Judy, and John Trent. *I'd Choose You* (Giving the Blessing to Your Child). Dallas: Word Publishing, 1994.

Magnus, Erica. *My Secret Place*. New York: Lothrop, Lee and Shepard Books, 1994.

Schloneger, Florence. *Sara's Trek*. Newton, Kansas: Faith & Life Press, 1981.

A word to parents and caregivers

The resources for children listed here are but a sample of many books that can help your child grow in faith and understanding. Enrich your children's lives with books. Read to them and let them read to you. Encourage quiet times. Emphasize and model the importance of reading and how it opens up a big, wide world for you and your children. Take time to visit bookstores. Browse in libraries for other resources. Encourage your children to go with you and allow them to select books. Make value decisions about books that will help your children in a variety of areas and encourage your children to do the same. Not all books may mention God, but if you look closely, you will repeatedly find good books that deal with issues related to biblical principles.

Index for Family Time

Index for Celebrate the Family

Index for Family Night Activities

General Index

About the Author

Anne Neufeld Rupp has written about parenting and family issues for nearly three decades. She has published more than 150 magazine and journal articles, several books, poems, songs, hymns, curriculum resources, and meditations.

An ordained minister who advocates for strong Christian education programs, she has been a regular contributor to several educational ministry periodicals, and wrote a monthly column on family issues for five years. Her experience includes pastoral ministry in two congregations, chaplaincy and program direction for a mental health facility, directing children's and adult choirs, and leading Christian education workshops.

Ann currently lives in Olathe, Kansas, with her computer programmer husband, Ken. For the past several years she has been a full-time free-lance writer and piano instructor.